Paris

IN

LOVE & LORE

A Guide to Romantic Hideaways,
Quirky Tales and Chic Escapes In and
Around Paris

CS WHITE

2025

Paris in Love & Lore

© 2025 CSW Studios LLC

First Edition

This book is intended as an inspirational and informational guide. While every effort has been made to ensure the accuracy of details at the time of publication, the author and publisher assume no responsibility for errors, omissions, or changes that may occur after printing. Travelers are encouraged to verify hours, access, and safety conditions independently.

The author and publisher shall not be held liable or responsible for any loss, injury, inconvenience, or damages incurred while using this book or visiting any locations mentioned herein. All experiences are undertaken at the reader's own discretion and risk.

About the Author

CS White has been in a love affair with Paris ever since she stepped off the plane as a teenage exchange student at fifteen. That first adventure sparked a lifelong passion for travel, culture, and connection—ultimately shaping a creative career that's taken her from globe-trotting in international business to designing beautiful spaces and now, writing unforgettable stories and guides.

Blending her deep affection for Paris with decades of experience in design and storytelling, Paris in Love & Lore marks her debut under her own name. With a sharp eye for style and a flair for finding magic in everyday moments, she invites readers into the romance, charm, and quirk of the City of Light.

Loving 'entrepreneurial location freedom,' she splits her time between New Orleans, coastal Florida, and Paris—often in the company of her brilliant partner, their blended and growing family, and two feisty dogs who believe they should always be at the center of the action.

When she's not writing or sketching out her next course for creative entrepreneurs, she's working on her first romance novel, coming in late 2025.

Follow along for travel stories, design tips, behind-the-scenes book updates, and a dash of everyday inspiration.

Contents

Strolls, stories, and secret corners made for hearts that wander.

Discover the most romantic spots in Paris—from moonlit bridges and hidden gardens to cozy cafés, cinematic kiss scenes, and timeless places where love lingers.

Curious characters, quirky tales, and the hidden pulse of Paris.

Explore the eccentric side of the city with bizarre history, unforgettable legends, and delightfully strange sites that most guidebooks leave behind.

Stylish homes, historic hideaways, and the interiors that define French flair.

Step inside (or hang out at the café across the street and imagine the interior) Paris's most elegant houses and nearby châteaux—spaces layered with design, drama, and delicious detail.

Introduction

Welcome to Paris in Love & Lore

There's something about Paris.

It seduces you slowly—through the scent of fresh bread on the morning air, a shimmer of light off the Seine, a quiet street corner that once played host to a love affair (or five). For me, the magic began at fifteen, stepping off a plane as a wide-eyed exchange student. I didn't know it then, but Paris would go on to shape not just my creative life—but my sense of beauty, curiosity, and the joy of a well-told story.

This book is a playful guide to the Paris you didn't know you needed—and to the readers who, like me, want more than a checklist of landmarks. You want the stories. The secrets. The soul of a place. You want Paris with personality.

So I've broken this book into three distinct sections:

Part I:
Romantic Paris

Think of this as your curated collection of swoon-worthy locations—both iconic and tucked-away gems—each steeped in its own romantic backstory or irresistible present-day charm. Perfect for proposals, dreamy walks, or just feeding your inner romantic with a croissant in hand.

A City for Lovers (and the Romantically Curious)

Paris didn't earn its nickname "The City of Love" by accident. It was whispered into being over candlelit dinners, scrawled in centuries-old love letters, and sealed with kisses beneath café awnings. But love here isn't just about grand gestures or cinematic kisses at the top of the Eiffel Tower. It's in the details: a shy glance on a footbridge, the scent of roses in a secret courtyard, a piano echoing through an open window on a rainy afternoon.

This section is your romantic treasure map.

Whether you're here on a honeymoon, a solo flirtation with the city, or dragging your partner on your twelfth visit (bless them), these 50 spots invite you to experience romance Paris-style: part history, part magic, always unforgettable.

What You'll Find Inside

Each location comes with a short and sweet story—some rooted in centuries-old history, others dripping with modern charm. You'll wander through moonlit gardens, discover tucked-away staircases perfect for a stolen kiss, and learn which bridge was once so covered in love locks it nearly collapsed under the weight of passion.

These aren't just places—they're settings. And you, dear reader, are the leading character.

Expect:

- A palace balcony with revolutionary gossip still echoing in the stonework.

- A 1920s bar where artists fell in love... and out of it.

- A little-known island that's basically Cupid's cul-de-sac.

Some spots are famous with a twist (yes, we're looking at you, Sacré-Cœur), while others might have you double-checking Google Maps to be sure they exist.

How to Use This Section

No one wants romance scheduled to the minute—so feel free to wander loosely. This isn't a race through monuments, it's a choose-your-own-love-story. Use this section to:

- Plan a perfect date, picnic, or proposal.

- Detour after your museum visit and stumble into a poetic corner of the city.

- Take a solo stroll and fall in love with Paris all over again.

You don't need to be in a relationship to enjoy this guide—Paris has always had a thing for passionate flâneurs, secret poets, and wide-eyed travelers. Bring your curiosity. Bring your heart. And maybe bring a bottle of wine.

Because in Paris, romance isn't just an event—it's the atmosphere.

* All addresses are documented and organized (by arrondissement, including metro stops) at the end of this section.

Themed Romantic Spots from Legendary to Low-Key

Seine-side Strolls

Explore romantic walks along the Seine's banks and bridges. From sunset strolls on storybook bridges to quiet islands in the river's embrace, this chapter highlights riverside rendezvous that have inspired lovers for centuries (think stolen kisses under a bridge and artists sketching their muses on the quais).

Pont Neuf (Bridge) – Despite its name meaning "New Bridge," Pont Neuf is Paris's oldest bridge and a timeless rendezvous spot for lovers. King Henry IV inaugurated it in 1607, and legend has it he enjoyed gallivanting around the nearby island so much that he earned the nickname "Vert- Galant" (the Green Gallant) for his amorous escapades. Today, couples linger along Pont Neuf's stone benches and watch boats glide by, basking in views of the Seine and the elegant facades of Île de la Cité. The bridge's sweeping vistas and central location have made it a backdrop for countless romantic moments on film and off – a place where historic charm and love flow together as smoothly as the river below.

Square du Vert-Galant (Riverside Garden) – Tucked at the tip of Île de la Cité, just below Pont Neuf, lies this little triangular park surrounded by the Seine's waters. Named after King Henry IV (yes, our "Green Gallant" himself), the square is a leafy oasis honoring the famously amorous king. A graceful weeping willow tree drapes over lovers on benches, and the gentle lapping of the river sets a soothing soundtrack. It's said that the Square du Vert-Galant's romantic reputation is so enduring that couples often descend here for picnics and proposals at sunset. With Paris's oldest bridge watching over and Tour boats coasting by, this spot feels like a secret garden afloat in the city – intimate, historical, and irresistibly romantic.

Pont Marie (Bridge) – Often nicknamed "lovers' bridge," Pont Marie comes with a charming tradition: if you kiss your sweetheart under its arches and make a wish, it just might come true. This 17th-century bridge connecting Île Saint-Louis to the Right Bank has seen centuries of couples float beneath it, hoping the Seine will carry their dreams downstream. There's no historical proof for the legend (even Wikipedia throws a bit of cold water on it), but why let facts spoil the fun? The bridge's serene views of Notre-Dame's towers and the stately townhouses of Île Saint-Louis certainly set a wish-worthy scene. Many newlyweds and lovers can't resist a smooch as they pass under Pont Marie on a boat cruise – after all, in the City of Love, a little magical thinking is par for the course.

Pont des Arts (Bridge) – Once upon a recent time, this elegant footbridge was so laden with tokens of love that it nearly collapsed under the weight of romance – literally. The Pont des Arts became famous for the thousands of "love locks" attached to its railings by couples sealing their love (keys tossed into the Seine for good measure). By 2015, Paris officials had to remove 45 tons of these padlocks after a section of the bridge's railing fell under their collective heft. Even without the locks, the Pont des Arts remains a beloved rendezvous spot, linking the Louvre to the Left Bank. It offers open-sky views of the river and landmarks, and often features impromptu music from street musicians serenading those who pause to admire the view. To this day, the bridge itself is a symbol of romance – proof that love, not metal, is what truly bridges people together (and it's a lot lighter on city infrastructure!).

Pont Alexandre III (Bridge) – Often hailed as Paris's most beautiful bridge, Pont Alexandre III is a Belle Époque masterpiece adorned with ornate lamp posts, golden-winged statues, and elaborate Art Nouveau flourishes. Spanning the Seine near Les Invalides and the Grand Palais, it's a favorite promenade for couples, especially at night when its lamps cast a soft glow on the gilt sculptures. Walking arm-in-arm here, you can almost hear the echoes of the 1900 World's Fair era when it was unveiled – a time of optimism, elegance, and perhaps a discreet rendezvous or two among Parisian high society. Pop culture has also cemented Alexandre III's romantic status: movie lovers might recall the dreamy final scene of Woody Allen's *Midnight in Paris* taking place on this very bridge, rain falling gently as two characters discover love in the Paris moonlight. Whether under sunshine or drizzle, Pont Alexandre III offers an ambiance that's equal parts grand romance and nostalgic charm.

Place Dauphine (Square) – One of Paris's most enchanting little squares, Place Dauphine sits quietly at the western end of Île de la Cité, forming a quaint triangle of calm in the city's heart. Bordered by 17th-century houses with rosy brick-and-stone facades, the square feels like a village hidden in plain sight. Many consider Place Dauphine one of the most romantic spots in Paris for its peaceful atmosphere and intimate scale. Historically, it was created under King Henri IV (he named it for his heir, the Dauphin), and over the centuries it has seen everything from fencing matches to artists' studios – surely with a fair share of love stories unfolding on its benches as well. Today, couples come here to sit beneath the chestnut trees or dine at one of the small cafés tucked in the corners. Away from the tourist bustle, Place Dauphine invites you to slow down and savor a very Parisian kind of romance: understated, elegant, and best enjoyed avec deux (with two).

Île Saint-Louis & Place Louis Aragon (Island & Riverside Spot) – Crossing onto Île Saint-Louis is like stepping back in time. This small island, largely unchanged since the 17th century, is a warren of narrow streets lined with graceful mansions, art galleries, and sweet shops. It's perfect for hand-in-hand wandering – perhaps with a stop for famous Berthillon ice cream to share. At the island's western tip, facing Notre-Dame, you'll find Place Louis Aragon, a tiny riverside square with a bench overlooking the water. This little spot is often blissfully uncrowded and offers lovely views of passing boats and the Gothic silhouette of Notre-Dame. It's easy to see why one travel writer calls it "the perfect place to sit for a snack and enjoy the views, or to enjoy a romantic moment at sunset." Fun fact: the square is named after Louis Aragon, a French poet whose verses about love and Paris are legendary – a fitting tribute as you whisper sweet words by the Seine.

Canal Saint-Martin (Waterway District) – For a different waterside vibe, the Canal Saint-Martin in northeastern Paris offers a trendy yet nostalgic backdrop for romance. Lined with iron footbridges and leafy trees, this 19th-century canal has a bohemian soul – one can easily imagine 19th-century lovers meeting secretly along its cobbled banks. In modern times, it's become a magnet for young Parisians; you'll find couples sharing a bottle of wine on the canal's edge or strolling past the quirky boutiques and cafés that now populate the neighborhood. The canal's poetic atmosphere caught the eye of filmmakers too: it was featured in the beloved French film

Amélie, where the heroine skips stones in the canal – a whimsical, heartwarming scene that encapsulates the area's charm. By day or night, Canal Saint-Martin feels authentic and intimate, an "old Paris" experience where you and your chéri(e) can walk locks and footbridges that seem made for two.

Hidden Courtyards and Whispered Secrets

Venture into secret gardens, tucked-away squares, and charming alleys off the tourist trail. These intimate spots (often known only to locals and savvy lovers) provide the perfect backdrop for quiet moments, sweet nothings, and perhaps a rendezvous fit for a 19th-century romance novel hero in disguise.

Place de Furstenberg (Hidden Square) – Tucked away in the chic Saint-Germain-des-Prés area, Place de Furstenberg is so tiny you might accidentally wander through it in seconds – but its charm will make you linger. This oval courtyard is lined with elegant buildings and anchored by an old-fashioned lamppost in the center, looking like a film set for a period romance. In fact, it has star quality: the painter Eugène Delacroix once had his studio here (now the Delacroix Museum), and legend has it that the soft, flattering light of Place de Furstenberg has inspired artists and lovers alike. With potted plants and climbing vines adding to the intimacy, it's often cited as a top proposal spot for those in-the-know. Come at dusk when the lamppost glows – you might feel you've slipped into a whispered conversation from a Balzac novel, or perhaps into the very last scene of a love story that's about to start anew.

Au Vieux Paris d'Arcole (Café) – Just a stone's throw from Notre-Dame, on a quiet side street, stands a postcard-perfect café draped seasonally in wisteria and charm. Au Vieux Paris d'Arcole is one of the oldest coffeehouses in the city (the building dates back to 1512!) and stepping inside or even just seeing its lavender-hued exterior feels like discovering a secret. In spring, cascades of purple wisteria blossoms tumble over its entrance, creating a natural love tunnel where couples pose for dreamy photos. Historically, this was once the rectory for the neighboring church – a dwelling for clergymen, ironically now a place devoted to earthly delights like good wine and tête-à-tête dinners. The interior is a cozy jumble of antique decor, but it's the quiet medieval street and that storybook façade that make hearts flutter. "Secret garden of wisteria" indeed – it's as if Cupid's personal decorator got loose in Paris.

Musée de la Vie Romantique (Museum) – With a name that literally translates to "Museum of Romantic Life," how could this place not be on a romance-themed tour? Hidden down a cobbled lane in Montmartre's foothills (9th arrondissement), this little museum is housed in a 19th-century mansion once owned by painter Ary Scheffer. In its heyday, Scheffer's home hosted salons frequented by the luminaries of the Romantic era – including writer George Sand and her then-lover, composer Frédéric Chopin. Imagine the candlelit evenings of music and poetry, with Chopin's notes in the air and Sand's deep laughter echoing in the halls. Today, the museum exhibits memorabilia of those Romantic age icons (paintings, letters, even a love letter or two perhaps), and there's a delightful garden café where you can sip tea under rose bushes. It's a tranquil refuge from the city's buzz – a place where art, literature, and love intertwine, transporting you to an era when "romantic" was a way of life. Don't be surprised if you leave inspired to pen a flowery sonnet for your cherie – or at least an artsy Instagram caption.

Galerie Vivienne (Covered Passage) – Paris's 19th-century covered passages are like early shopping malls crossed with secret tunnels – and Galerie Vivienne is arguably the most beautiful of them all. Tucked near the Palais Royal, this elegant, covered arcade features mosaic-tiled floors, a glass-paned roof that filters in dreamy light, and boutique storefronts that have remained largely unchanged for over a century. In its Victorian-era prime, dandies and ladies would stroll these passages arm in arm, sheltered from rain and prying eyes alike. Today, couples can do the same: window-shop old books and wines, duck into a quaint bistro, or simply meander through, admiring the Neo-classical decor. With its quiet corners and old-world elegance, Galerie Vivienne feels like a portal to the past. One can easily fantasize about a clandestine 1830s rendezvous here – perhaps Balzac meeting a secret lover by the bookshop, or Colette (who once had a boutique here) exchanging flirtatious banter with a muse. It's the perfect hideaway when you want Paris romance without the crowds, a little whisper of "la vie Parisienne" under a glass sky.

Village Saint-Paul (Courtyards) – In the heart of the Marais, behind a maze of stone walls and gateways, lies Village Saint-Paul – a series of connected courtyards that form an antique dealers' enclave by day and a fairy-lit ghost village by night. Wandering here feels like discovering a forgotten world. By daylight, you'll find vintage shops and art galleries; by evening, the courtyards grow hushed, and old lamps cast long shadows on the cobblestones. It's wonderfully atmospheric and often nearly empty except for the occasional cat slinking by. Historically, this area was part of a medieval village and later the courtyard of a royal palace (Queen Margot's digs – if walls could talk!). Today it's a haven for those seeking a quiet romantic stroll. If you two are the type who bond over hidden history and treasure hunting, you'll adore peeking into the nooks here. Come twilight, when doors close and silence descends, you can slow-dance under a balcony or simply enjoy the luxury of having a secret slice of Paris all to yourselves.

Square Saint-Gilles-du-Grand-Veneur (Hidden Garden) –
This little-known square in the Haut Marais wins the prize for most
hyphenated name and perhaps most unexpectedly romantic
hideaway. Tucked behind an unassuming archway on Rue de Hesse,
Square Saint-Gilles-du-Grand-Veneur is a small garden famed for its
rose bushes and the picture-perfect view of a historic hôtel particulier
(mansion) façade. In summer, the roses climb trellises, creating a
fragrant haven that feels far removed from urban bustle. It's a
popular spot for engagement photo shoots – walk in and you might
spot a blissful couple being directed by a photographer as they
canoodle among the blooms. The square's very existence feels
secretive; many Parisians don't even know it's there. This only adds
to the appeal for lovebirds seeking solitude. Pack a pastry, sit on a
bench, and pretend this is your private garden in Paris – save for
perhaps a shy local or two who know they've stumbled on something
special, much like you have.

Promenade Plantée (Garden Walkway) – Long before New
York had the High Line, Paris converted an old railway into an
elevated garden path known as La Promenade Plantée (or Coulée
Verte). Stretching nearly 3 miles from Bastille into the east of Paris,
this lush walkway is lined with flowers, shrubs, and arbors that create
little green archways – ideal for a leisurely stroll with your
amoureux(se). One moment you're above streets and viaducts,
catching glimpses of rooftops; the next, the path dips through a
tunnel of bamboo or past a trickling fountain. Opened in 1993, it was
the first project of its kind and remains a favorite for those in the
know. There's something inherently romantic about repurposing old
tracks – a symbol of journeys – into a garden path, as if saying every
old route can find new purpose (much like old love can blossom

anew). If your feet get tired, find a secluded bench surrounded by climbing roses and let the gentle sway of the remaining train signal posts (now decorated with vines) take you back in time. It's Paris's secret rooftop garden, perfect for love to quietly bloom.

Rue de l'Abreuvoir & La Maison Rose (Street & Café) – In Montmartre's labyrinth of picturesque lanes, Rue de l'Abreuvoir stands out as one of the most romantic streets in the city. Winding down a gentle slope toward the vineyards, this cobbled street is lined with storybook houses – none more iconic than La Maison Rose, a small corner café painted in rosy pink. This spot has been immortalized in paintings and Instagram feeds alike for its candy-colored walls and green shutters, often adorned with trailing ivy. In the early 20th century, artists like Picasso and Utrillo frequented La Maison Rose; one can only imagine the bohemian romances kindled over absinthe or coffee in its quaint interior. Today, couples pose outside to capture that quintessential Montmartre magic, or they sit at a sidewalk table to watch the world (and maybe a film crew) go by. At the top of Rue de l'Abreuvoir stands a bust of Dalida, the beloved French singer, who made Montmartre her home – fittingly, her statue is said to bring luck in love to those who touch it (or so locals joke). Wandering here, it's easy to feel transported to a village in the countryside. Fewer crowds venture this far uphill, so you and your sweetheart might have a rare moment of Montmartre tranquility, with only the ghosts of artists past to eavesdrop on your murmured sweet nothings.

Le Mur des "Je t'aime" (I Love You Wall, Art Installation) – Tucked in a small garden square in Montmartre (Square Jehan Rictus, near Abbesses), you'll find one of Paris's most overt declarations of love: Le Mur des Je t'aime. This modern mural is a 40-

square-meter wall composed of 612 blue enamel tiles, on which the phrase "I love you" is written 311 times in 250 different languages. It's essentially the world's largest love letter. Created in 2000 by artists Frédéric Baron and Claire Kito, the wall was born from Baron's quest to gather "I love you" in every language – a mission he accomplished by knocking on embassies and chatting with neighbors around the world. The result is a global testament to love, with every dialect from French to Navajo to Esperanto represented. Couples flock here to find their mother tongue on the wall and snap a photo (engagement selfies galore). The wall even has red splashes on it – symbolizing pieces of a broken heart that, in the artists' vision, the wall brings back together. Corny? Perhaps. But standing before it, shoulder to shoulder with someone special, you can't help but feel the warm, fuzzy universality of love. It's a must-see for romantics – a spot where je t'aime is literally written in stone (or tile, in this case).

Clos Montmartre (Vineyard) – Vineyards in Paris? Oui, and Montmartre's got one! Tucked behind the Montmartre Museum on a steep hillside is Le Clos Montmartre, a tiny working vineyard that has been producing wine since the 1930s (though wine on this hill goes back to the Abbesses nuns in the Middle Ages). It's a delightful anomaly – rows of grapevines growing in the shadow of Sacré-Cœur and Moulin de la Galette's windmill. While the vineyard itself is fenced off to protect the precious grapes, you can peek in from Rue des Saules or the terraces above. There's a certain romance to stumbling upon grapevines in the city: a reminder of Montmartre's village past when this was a rural hamlet of windmills, guinguettes (open-air taverns), and cheeky cancan dancers. Each October, Montmartre even hosts a Wine Harvest Festival, a joyful celebration with parades and fireworks, honoring the new vintage – a tradition that brings the whole neighborhood (and lots of visitors) together in merriment. Perhaps it's the wine talking, but the festival has seen its share of flirtations and maybe a proposal or two under the vines. Even on a quiet day, the view of Clos Montmartre is whimsical and heartwarming. It shows that even in a metropolis, there's room for little miracles of greenery and tradition – much like love finding a way to thrive in unlikely places.

Enchanted Gardens of Love

Discover Paris's parks and gardens where romance blossoms among fountains and flowerbeds. From royal gardens where queens once flirted with suitors, to rustic parks where modern couples picnic and daydream, this chapter paints Paris's green spaces as leafy love nests across history and today.

Luxembourg Gardens (Park) – The Jardin du Luxembourg is the grande dame of Parisian parks – elegant, inviting, and brimming with romance. Commissioned in the 17th century by Queen Marie de Medici, these gardens were designed to remind her of her native Florence (hence the Italianate palace and Medici Fountain within). Today, the Luxembourg is beloved by all, but there's a special magic here for couples. Perhaps it's the Grand Basin Pond where you can sail little boats (or watch children do it, while daydreaming of your own happily-ever-after). Perhaps it's the secluded arbors and alleys of lime trees that create natural canopies perfect for strolling arm in arm. Literary love has roots here too: Victor Hugo set the budding romance of Marius and Cosette *in Les Misérables* amidst the Luxembourg's very paths – "we experience Marius's falling in love with Cosette in the Luxembourg Gardens as she and her Papa sit on a bench each day by a gladiator statue," one scholar notes. Real-life couples often follow suit, occupying the iconic green chairs around the fountain or cuddling by the Medici Fountain, where a dramatic statue of the cyclops Polyphemus surprising lovers Acis and Galatea adds mythic passion to the scene. On a sunny day, the air is filled with the scent of flowers and often the melodies of a lone violinist. It's le fabuleux destin (the fabulous fate) of this garden to be a stage for love stories old and new.

Tuileries Garden (Park) – Stretching between the Louvre and Place de la Concorde, the Tuileries is Paris's central showcase garden – once the royal family's backyard, now every romantic's playground. Designed by the king of Baroque gardening, André Le Nôtre, its broad gravel promenades and geometric flowerbeds give it a regal feel. Yet, it's equally a place of simple pleasures: couples lounge together by the round ponds, maybe with a gelato in hand, or they meander through the lanes of statues (Cupid and psyche here, a passionate Rodin sculpture there). In summer, a Ferris wheel often graces the edge of the Tuileries. A shared gondola ride gives a thrilling, if momentary, bird's-eye view of Paris – an experience one guide describes as "very special... lovely views & solitude on the Ferris wheel," especially if you get a cart all to yourselves. As evening falls, the garden's vibe shifts from lively to languid; the crowds thin, and you might find yourselves nearly alone under the alignments of trees, with the Louvre's silhouette watching over. It's easy to imagine the echoes of bygone aristocrats whispering sweet French nothings as they stole away from courtly duties for a private stroll. In the Tuileries, every couple can feel a bit like royalty amid the romance.

Parc des Buttes-Chaumont (Park) – For those willing to venture beyond the tourist center, Buttes- Chaumont offers a dramatic sort of romance – both geographically and emotionally. Built in 1867 on what used to be a stone quarry (and execution ground, if we go further back – but let's focus on the love!), this park in northeast Paris is all rolling hills, cliffs, and surprises. At its heart is a deep lake spanned by a suspension bridge (where a smooch mid-bridge will definitely give you butterflies, thanks to the gentle sway). Perched high on a rocky crag is the Temple de la Sibylle, a tiny Corinthian temple modelled after one in Italy – it's basically a mini "temple of love" with one of the best panoramas of the city around. Many a proposal has happened up there, with the distant Sacré- Cœur dome as witness. The park's winding paths through groves of trees can feel almost wild and secluded – perfect for couples seeking a bit of nature and privacy. In nice weather, you'll spot pairs lying on the grass or sharing a picnic, looking blissfully far from urban worries. Buttes-Chaumont has a local, authentic feel and even a touch of bohemian history (nearby, the 19th-century Communards plotted revolution). Today, it mostly plots romance: just ask anyone who's sat by the waterfall grotto or under a blossoming tree here – it's très romantique.

Parc Monceau (Park) – Parc Monceau is the definition of a romantic urban park on a boutique scale. Nestled in a chic residential area of the 8th arrondissement, Monceau was landscaped in the 18th century as a whimsical English-style garden, complete with follies (faux Roman columns, an Egyptian pyramid, even a little Venetian bridge). The result is a park that feels at once curated and a little dreamy. Claude Monet painted it, writers from Marcel Proust to Sidonie-Gabrielle Colette strolled it, and today couples in love frequent it – especially locals who know its charms. Imagine a leisurely walk around the oval path, passing a reflection pond with weeping willows trailing their branches into the water. Each turn might reveal a surprise – a Renaissance archway here, a grotto there. With fewer tourists, Parc Monceau often provides a more private atmosphere for a tête-à-tête on a bench. Fun historical tidbit: in the 1770s, this park was the site of lavish fêtes thrown by the Duke of Chartres, including the first hot air balloon flight with passengers (a sheep, a duck, and a rooster – not exactly romantic, but delightfully odd!). These days, the only airborne creatures are pigeons and the occasional kite, but the park's gentle, timeless vibe makes it a lovely spot to let your hearts float freely.

Parc de Bagatelle (Garden) – Hidden within the sprawling Bois de Boulogne on Paris's western edge, the Bagatelle Gardens are a floral paradise born of a romantic wager. Legend says that in 1778, Queen Marie-Antoinette bet her brother-in-law, the Count of Artois, that he couldn't build a splendid palace and garden in under three months. He delivered: Château de Bagatelle (meaning a "trifle" or "little nothing") and its surrounding gardens were completed in 64 days – and they are très magnifique. Today, Bagatelle is especially famous for its rose garden, boasting thousands of rose bushes of countless varieties. Visit in late spring or early summer, and you'll be enveloped in a heady perfume as you wander among blossoms of every hue, each romantically named ("Belle de Bagatelle," "Souvenir de la Malmaison"). It's a popular site for wedding photos – you might glimpse a bride and groom wandering like characters from a Jane Austen novel. Peacocks strut around the lawns, adding a fairytale feel (and occasionally squawking at just the wrong moment, to humorous effect). With its little bridges, lily pond, and even a whimsical pagoda, Parc de Bagatelle invites lovers to get delightfully lost. Pack a picnic and clink champagne flutes in this secret garden; after all, it was literally built on a dare to create something beautiful fast – proof that where there's a will (and a royal whim), romance finds a way.

Jardin du Palais-Royal (Courtyard Garden) – Few places marry history and romance as effortlessly as the Palais-Royal gardens. Tucked behind a grand palace (which was once Cardinal Richelieu's residence and later a royal abode), this enclosed garden feels like a world unto itself. Elegant 18th- century arcades line the sides, housing art galleries and cafés. In the center: a formal garden with manicured trees, fountains, and colorful flowerbeds. But don't let the symmetry fool you – the Palais- Royal has always had a cheeky, subversive side. In the 1780s it was a notorious hotspot for clandestine encounters, gambling, and other pleasures (mischievous pamphleteer Restif de la Bretonne dubbed it "the capital of Paris"). Today's pursuits are tamer, but a whiff of that free-spirited past lingers, giving the romance here an extra spice. Modern art installations – like Daniel Buren's striped black-and-white columns – provide playful spots for couples to perch and people-watch. On a sunny afternoon, you'll see Parisians of all ages lounging by the central fountain, lovers flirting over coffee at the famed Café Kitsuné, and perhaps even an impromptu tango under the colonnades. Come evening, when the crowds thin, the garden's lamps cast a golden glow and the scene practically screams "propose now!" if you haven't already. Audrey Hepburn and Cary Grant strolled these grounds in *Charade* – and indeed, the Jardin du Palais-Royal remains ever ready for its close-up as a setting for love.

Bois de Boulogne Lake (Rowboat Experience) – Once upon a time, the Bois de Boulogne was the royal hunting ground – fast forward and it's now a vast park where Parisians go to relax, play, and yes, woo. Deep within this "forest" on the city's outskirts lies a charming little lake by the name of Lac Inférieur, where one can hire a rowboat by the hour. Gliding across the water with your beloved as you row under arched bridges and past wooded islets is about as storybook-romantic as it gets. In fact, one travel guide suggests on a warm day you "hire a boat on the lake… and why not bring a picnic" to complete the scene. The act of rowing your love around recalls poetic images from centuries past (perhaps a dapper gent in a boater hat, singing an aria to his belle – or at least sharing a laugh as he clumsily paddles). Surrounding you are swans, ducks, and the rustling leaves of the Bois; it's easy to forget you're right on the edge of a bustling metropolis. Many couples cap this experience by spreading a blanket on the grassy banks afterward, clinking plastic wine glasses, and toasting to the serene escapade. Sure, you might briefly debate who rowed better, but in the end, it's all la vie en rose on this tranquil lake – a Parisian twist on the classic "rowboat romance" scene.

Dining à Deux

Savor the art of dining with a side of seduction. This chapter guides readers through candlelit bistros, Belle Époque restaurants, and cozy cafés steeped in history. Each venue comes with its own delectable tales of famous lovers, clandestine trysts in private booths, or simply an ambiance so magical that even the menu seems written in the language of love. These may not be new finds, but you may be surprised by their interesting histories.

Le Jules Verne (Restaurant) – Elevate your dinner – literally – at Le Jules Verne, the Michelin-starred restaurant perched on the Eiffel Tower's second level. This is the kind of once-in-a-lifetime venue that practically comes with its own romance soundtrack. As you ride a private lift up the Iron Lady's leg, butterflies flutter (in your stomach, not just around the Tower). The dining room offers panoramic windows framing glittering views of Paris below; by night, the city twinkles and every hour the tower itself sparkles, making you feel like you're inside a champagne flute. The cuisine is haute French, the service top-notch, and proposals here are so frequent that the staff probably have a protocol for bringing the ring in the dessert. It's undeniably pricey – one travel blog wryly notes the "price corresponds" to the unforgettable experience – but for many, this is the splurge for a romantic Paris trip. Fun fact: one famous engagement here was actor Tom Cruise popping the question to Katie Holmes at the summit of the tower. And if that love story didn't last, fear not – the legend of the Eiffel Tower's magic endures. Dining at Le Jules Verne is to taste Paris from the sky, where every bite and every glance out the window feels like an extravagant celebration of l'amour.

Lapérouse (Restaurant) – Lapérouse isn't just a restaurant; it's practically a museum of scandalous romance. Established in 1766 on the Quai des Grands Augustins, this restaurant gained notoriety in the 19th century for its private dining salons where powerful men would entertain their mistresses away from prying eyes. These sumptuous little rooms still exist, complete with Belle Époque decor – and most famously, mirrors covered in scratches. Why is it scratched? Because those mistresses (known as cocottes) wanted to test if the diamonds they were given were real – so they'd try to etch the glass with them! If the mirror scratched, the gem was genuine... and the gentleman's love (or guilt) was proven true. The mirrors at Lapérouse still bear hundreds of these marks – graffiti of passion and materialism that has become legendary. Today, Lapérouse has been refurbished and remains a den of romance and fine dining, with dim lighting, plush velvet seating, and an aura of naughty glamour. It's said that writer Victor Hugo, artist Gustave Flaubert, and even Napoleon III were patrons. Modern couples can reserve those very salons (with discreet service via a hidden cupboard, as was done in old times) for an exceptionally intimate dinner. Dining here, one can't help but feel the thrill of its history – the clandestine whispers of lovers past – adding spice to the meal. Just resist the urge to add your own scratch to the mirror; better to let your sparkling conversation be proof enough of love.

Le Coupe-Chou (Restaurant) – Tucked away on a medieval street of the Latin Quarter, Le Coupe- Chou is the kind of restaurant that seems torn from the pages of The Three Musketeers. It occupies a collection of 14th-century stone cottages, complete with crackling fireplaces, wooden beams, and an assortment of vintage armchairs that invite you to sink in for hours. The name means "the cabbage-cutter," but fear not, nothing violent here – it's all about cozy charm. This is a go-to spot for a quiet, intimate dinner, especially on a chilly evening when the fireplace is lit, casting flickers on the old stone walls. Candlelight, hearty French fare (boeuf bourguignon, anyone?), and perhaps a bottle of Bordeaux set the scene for deep conversation and stolen kisses between courses. Many students from the nearby Sorbonne have fallen in love over dessert here – or at least fallen in love with the chocolate mousse. With multiple snug rooms and nooks, Le Coupe-Chou almost gives the feeling you have the place to yourselves, even if other diners are around the corner. It's relatively affordable and low-key, proving that a meal doesn't need Eiffel Tower views to be utterly romantic. In fact, one could imagine a penniless poet impressing his muse here more than at any palatial dining room. The Coupe-Chou shows that sometimes romance favors the simple, the rustic, and the genuine.

Le Procope (Café/Restaurant) – As the oldest café in Paris (est. 1686!), Le Procope has seen a lot in its 300+ years: revolutionaries plotting, philosophers debating, and likely a secret tête-à-tête or two in shadowy corners. Tucked in Saint-Germain, the Procope's walls are lined with portraits of Voltaire, Rousseau, and other Enlightenment thinkers who sipped coffee (and likely flirted with witty salonnières) here. Voltaire supposedly drank 40 cups a day – though perhaps it was the charming company that truly kept him awake. Today, Le Procope is more of a restaurant than a café, but it retains its 18th-century elegance with chandeliers, marble tables, and servers in period-esque attire. Dining here is like stepping back in time; you half expect Mozart to waltz in or Napoleon (an early patron) to hand his hat to the cloakroom – actually, his hat is on display on the wall! For couples, Le Procope offers a chance to dine enveloped in history. Discussing ideas by candlelight over coq au vin and crème brûlée can feel intellectually titillating – very "dangerous liaisons" vibes. And if your date happens to be a history buff or literature lover, brownie points: you're literally feasting where literary and political love affairs once unfolded. The occasional tongue-in-cheek thought might cross your mind – would Jean-Jacques Rousseau approve of my wine choice? – But the best advice here is simply to soak up the ambiance. In the very spot where Benjamin Franklin once talked revolution, you can toast to la révolution d'amour – the personal little revolution of being blissfully, deliciously in love in Paris.

Maxim's (Restaurant) – If Belle Époque Paris had a clubhouse for the glamorous and amorous, Maxim's would be it. Established in 1893 and still preserving its Art Nouveau splendor, this legendary restaurant in the 8th arrondissement was the hub of high society gatherings at the turn of the 20th century. Think mirrored walls, red velvet, Tiffany lamps – the works. It was so famous for illicit romantic liaisons that it became a setting for the musical *Gigi*, where a young Louis Jourdan sings about the women at Maxim's in one memorable scene. The joke back then was, if you sat by Maxim's windows, you might catch a gent with his wife on one side and his mistress on the other, each pretending not to see the other. Nowadays, Maxim's is a bit of a time capsule and tourist draw, but its aura of naughty elegance remains. The menu is classic French (and expensive – many a swain probably had to pawn a tie pin to pay the bill in days of yore). But for couples who adore Art Nouveau or want to reenact the extravagance of la belle vie, an evening at Maxim's is a bucket-list experience. The dance hall upstairs even hosts period-themed dinner shows occasionally, reviving the spirit of the Can-Can and French Cancan. Dress up to the nines, channel your inner Coco Chanel or Duke, and swirl that Champagne. In Maxim's gilt-edged mirrors, you'll see not only yourselves but perhaps the faint reflection of courtesans and counts waltzing behind you — the ghosts of romance past, giving an approving nod.

La Tour d'Argent (Restaurant) – Overlooking the Seine with a direct view of Notre-Dame, La Tour d'Argent (dating back to 1582) oozes history and refinement. This is where kings, celebrities, and discerning lovebirds have dined for centuries. Its claim to fame? Legendary pressed duck and an even more legendary wine cellar – but beyond gastronomy, it's the sense of occasion that makes Tour d'Argent special for romance. The dining room, high up with those river views, is all white tablecloths and silver cloches; an army of attentive staff ensure you feel like royalty on a state dinner. It's said that in the past, gentlemen would carve their initials into the window frames when proposing here (which, if true, makes one worry about the state of the frames!). One quirky tradition: every duck served is numbered – they've been doing this since 1890, and the numbers are in the millions now. Imagine telling your grandchildren "Your grandma and I shared pressed duck number 1,234,567 at Tour d'Argent." If that's not an anecdote for the ages, what is? While formal, the restaurant has appeared in pop culture with surprisingly cute effect – it inspired the restaurant in Pixar's Ratatouille. So if a rat could find love and purpose in a Parisian kitchen, surely human couples can manage a bit of romance over fine wine and foie gras. Dining here is a splurge, but one that creates a vivid memory: the night you felt transported to an era of elegance, clinking glasses as the Seine shimmered and Notre-Dame stood guardian to your love.

Le Train Bleu (Restaurant) – All aboard for a journey to the golden age of travel romance! Le Train Bleu is a jaw-droppingly ornate restaurant inside the Gare de Lyon train station, and walking into it feels like stepping onto a luxury railway carriage of the 1900s – only it doesn't move, which is better for soup consumption. The interior is a riot of Belle Époque frescoes, gilded moldings, giant chandeliers – in short, pure drama. It was originally the station buffet for travelers heading to the Riviera, so you can imagine elegant couples in 1901 stopping here for a last steak au poivre before catching the night train to Nice, perhaps eloping or honeymooning. Today, it's open to all, no ticket needed, and remains a fabulous spot for a romantic meal with a side of time travel. Slide into the leather banquette, order something classic (the roast lamb leg carved tableside is theater in itself), and soak up the atmosphere as trains quietly rumble in the station below. Many a film has used Le Train Bleu as a backdrop (like Mr. Bean's Holiday and Nikita), but it doesn't overshadow real-life romance. There's something about being in a train station – even a stationary part of it – that gives a sense of adventure. Maybe after dessert you'll feel inspired to impulsively hop on a midnight train to Venice? Or more realistically, you'll step out into Paris's night feeling like you just dined in a living painting. Either way, Le Train Bleu promises a first-class journey for the heart, no passport required.

Le Grand Véfour (Restaurant) – Nestled in the arcades of the Palais-Royal, Le Grand Véfour is not just a restaurant; it's a living monument to French gastronomy and romance. This two-Michelin-star gem has been serving fine cuisine since 1784, and its dining room still gleams with Empire-era mirrors, painted cherubs on the ceiling, and plush velvet banquettes. Those banquettes have held some notable derrières: Napoleon Bonaparte and Joséphine dined here (legend says it's even where Napoleon proposed marriage to his Josephine!), as did Victor Hugo, Colette, and Sartre and Simone de Beauvoir in later years. In fact, many seats bear little plaques with illustrious names – so you might literally sit where Jean Cocteau or Mistinguett once canoodled. Despite the luxe setting, the space is intimate and hushed – it feels like a jewel box hidden away from the world. The restaurant's very location, overlooking the tranquil Palais-Royal garden, means a post-dinner moonlit stroll under those arched pathways is a must – perhaps to walk off the exquisite meal and whisper about how you just dined in the same spot as 200 years of lovers and luminaries. A meal at Le Grand Véfour is a splurge of the highest order, but it's also a few hours living in a dream. As you clink glasses and taste the art on the plate, you become part of its storied history. And if you're really moved by the spirit, maybe you'll drop to one knee among the porcelain and crystal – after all, if it was good enough for Napoleon...

Café de Flore (Café) – Few cafes have the mythic romantic status of Café de Flore in Saint-Germain-des-Prés. It's not that the waiters are especially tender (they're classically brusque) or that the coffee is life-changing (it's good, but coffee is coffee). It's the aura – decades of intellectuals, artists, and their lovers converged here, making it a symbol of Left Bank romance and bohemian chic. Most famously, philosopher Jean-Paul Sartre and writer Simone de Beauvoir practically lived at Flore in the 1940s, spending countless hours in its red booths in a passionate partnership of minds and hearts. Their presence helped make Flore world-famous, and the cafe happily claims them (along with Hemingway and others) as its own. Today, sitting in Café de Flore, you can channel that energy. Sure, there are tourists snapping pics of the art deco sign, but there are also genuine Parisian couples reading poetry books together or an old man with a rose secretly waiting for his chère amie. Grab a spot upstairs if you can (it's quieter), order a rich chocolat chaud or a glass of Saint-Germain wine, and let time slow down. It's the kind of place where you can have deep 2 a.m. conversations about life, or flirt playfully while people-watching the boulevard. The price of your coffee buys you a piece of Parisian legend: you're in the same setting where one of the greatest love stories of intellect and devotion, Sartre & Beauvoir's, played out in real life. In that light, the bill suddenly feels like a bargain.

La Closerie des Lilas (Brasserie & Piano Bar) – Down in Montparnasse, La Closerie des Lilas has been the haunt of lovers and literati since the 19th century. This is where Hemingway wrote parts of *The Sun Also Rises* (his favorite seat is marked with a plaque), and where he also drank with Fitzgerald, likely discussing matters of love and prose. The Closerie retains a velvety, intimate vibe: dark wood interiors, an old piano tinkling jazz tunes in the corner, and a leafy outdoor terrace for summer nights. It's both a brasserie (more casual dining) and a cocktail bar, so you can adapt your romantic encounter accordingly. Many a date in Paris begins or ends at the Closerie's bar, with its famous cocktails bearing names of artists – perhaps you'll toast with a "Poète" or "Apollinaire." The atmosphere invites confidences: it was true for the famous folks (Fitzgerald allegedly had a meltdown here after hearing his novel wasn't selling – only to be comforted by drink and friends) and it's true for couples today. Something about the Closerie's warmth and the ghosts of creative giants loosens tongues and heartstrings. By the time you're sharing a profiterole or swaying to a live pianist's rendition of "La Vie en Rose," you might just believe that some of that genius and romance has rubbed off on you, too. At the very least, you're following in illustrious footsteps – and what's more romantic than feeling part of a grand tradition of love and art?

Bel Canto (Restaurant/Cabaret) – Dinner and a show, with a twist: at Bel Canto in the Marais, your waiters are the show. This unique restaurant pairs fine French dining with live opera performances by the serving staff, who are all trained opera singers. One minute they're pouring your Bordeaux, the next they burst into a Verdi aria inches from your table. The result is surprisingly magical – even for those who don't know their Puccini from their Pavarotti. The intimacy of the venue means these performances feel like a personal serenade. Imagine a tenor belting "La donna è mobile" while you twirl spaghetti, or a soprano delivering a heart-melting "O mio babbino caro" as you stare into your partner's eyes over dessert. You might get chills (from the music, not the ice cream). The concept was, as one article notes, to give guests the impression of "dining on stage" – and indeed, it's an immersive experience that often leaves couples beaming. Historically, opera and romance go hand in hand (with a fair share of tragedy in those plotlines, but we'll ignore that). Here, you get the passion of opera without anyone dramatically dying at the end – quite the opposite, you're likely to walk out feeling uplifted. Bel Canto proves that in Paris, even a meal can be an affair of the heart, complete with a soundtrack worthy of a love story.

Historic Love Stories in Stone and Canvas

Time-travel through the city's museums, monuments, and churches to uncover the great love stories and romantic legends behind the art and architecture. Readers will encounter sculptures of smitten gods, paintings of star-crossed lovers, a wall that says "I love you" in 250 languages, and even the tombs and landmarks where Paris's real-life lovers and fictional sweethearts made history.

Notre-Dame Cathedral (Cathedral) – Few monuments have witnessed as many declarations of love (and perhaps a few tearful breakups) as Notre-Dame de Paris. For over 850 years, this Gothic masterpiece has stood on the Île de la Cité, its flying buttresses and gargoyles silently observing the ebb and flow of lovers in its shadow. The cathedral itself has a romantic soul: think of Quasimodo pining for Esmeralda in Victor Hugo's novel, giving us the archetype of the tragic, devoted lover. In real life, countless couples have met on its parvis (the wide plaza out front), perhaps rendezvousing by the statue of Charlemagne, or agreed to marry after climbing its narrow spiral stairs and feeling on top of the world. Trolling around the edifice at night, with its stained-glass windows dark but the memory of their glow alive, is undeniably atmospheric. Many a Parisian engagement has taken place with Notre-Dame's façade as the grand witness. And don't forget Point Zero in the square – the bronze star marking the center of Paris from which all distances in France are measured. There's a tradition that couples who step on it will return to Paris together (some say it grants a wish). True or not, it's a charming ritual to do hand-in-hand. Notre-Dame is, in many ways, the heart of Paris – and what is that if not a symbol of love's endurance against all odds?

Sainte-Chapelle (Chapel) – A short stroll from Notre-Dame, tucked within the Palais de Justice complex, Sainte-Chapelle is a jewel-box of a chapel that can set any heart aflutter. Built in the 1240s by King Louis IX to house holy relics (talk about a passionate endeavor), this Gothic chapel's upper floor is encased in 15 soaring stained-glass windows that bathe the interior in a kaleidoscope of colors. Stepping inside is like walking into a wedding cake made of light. It's intimate, ethereal, and undeniably romantic – so much so that proposals have been known to occur spontaneously in the presence of such beauty (though one should be mindful of the other tourists!). Each stained-glass pane tells a story, and many are biblical – but one can imagine they also secretly chronicle the tales of devotion of the craftsmen who made them. Modern visitors often stand in awe, hand in hand, heads tilted up to the rainbow heavens. By evening, when classical music concerts are held here, the ambiance becomes even more sublime. Listening to Vivaldi or Pachelbel's Canon in D in this hallowed space with your beloved beside you might just redefine "date night." If Notre-Dame is Paris's grand heart, Sainte-Chapelle is its soulful, delicate heartbeat – quieter but deeply affecting. It's the kind of place where you whisper "I love you" almost automatically, perhaps because the very air seems to whisper it back.

The Louvre Museum (Museum) – The Louvre is often celebrated for its art, but it's also a place of myriad love stories – on the canvases, among the sculptures, and even in its very halls. As a former royal palace, it saw plenty of royal romances (and scandals) within its walls long before it was a museum. Walking through its galleries, you'll encounter depictions of love in all forms: Psyche Revived by Cupid's Kiss, a marble sculpture by Canova, captures the very moment of love's awakening with breathtaking tenderness – one can't help but sigh seeing Cupid revive his beloved. There's the famous painting of The Coronation of Napoleon, where Napoleon crowns Joséphine Empress – a scene of power, yes, but also of his love and ambition entwined (his letters to Joséphine, found elsewhere, were steamy enough to fog the Mona Lisa's glass). The very architecture of the Louvre carries echoes of romance: the Richelieu wing features salons where Napoleon III hosted opulent balls, and where his flirtatious wife Eugénie charmed dignitaries. Today, the Tuileries Garden just outside is a haven for couples' post-museum stroll, where they process the art and perhaps sneak a kiss by the pyramid reflecting pool. A fun anecdote: the Louvre's most famous resident, Mona Lisa, has her own love lore – some say her smile was because she was secretly pregnant, glowing with maternal love; others say da Vinci hired musicians to keep her entertained (and smiling) as he painted, essentially wooing that expression out of her. Whether or not that's true, the Louvre certainly provides endless conversation starters for partners ("So, how about that Venus de Milo? Would you still love me if I had no arms?"). It's a place to be intellectually and visually stimulated together – and isn't intellectual foreplay just the cherry on top of Parisian romance?

Musée Rodin (Museum & Garden) – If there's one artist who captured passion in stone, it's Auguste Rodin. The Musée Rodin, set in a serene mansion and garden where the sculptor once worked, is practically a sanctuary of sensuality. At the center of it all is The Kiss – Rodin's famous marble sculpture of two lovers entwined, lips inches apart – arguably one of the most romantic artworks ever created. Strolling through the rose-filled gardens, you'll encounter this sculpture and many others, like Eternal Springtime (another ode to love) and The Thinker (okay, more pensive, but perhaps pondering love lost?). Rodin's own love life was dramatic: his muse and lover, Camille Claudel, was a brilliant sculptor herself, and their tempestuous affair is the stuff of legend. In these gardens, it's easy to imagine their ghosts – she passionately critiquing a half-finished sculpture, he equally passionately trying to steal a kiss. The mansion's interiors showcase letters and works that hint at the fervor of their bond. For modern visitors, the Musée Rodin is a quieter gem away from the big crowds – couples often find a shaded bench to sit and admire the view of Les Invalides' golden dome, or they playfully mimic the poses of the sculptures for fun selfies. The fragrant roses (often in bloom in summer) and the hushed gravel paths set a perfect stage for romance. It's no surprise that this museum sees its fair share of proposals too; who could resist saying yes with The Kiss as a witness?

Musée d'Orsay (Museum) – Housed in a former Beaux-Arts railway station, the Musée d'Orsay is often considered one of the most beautiful museums in the world – and beauty and love tend to go hand in hand. The collection is a treasure trove of 19th-century art, featuring numerous romantic and sensual works. Stroll with your partner through the Impressionist galleries and you'll find Renoir's Dance at Le Moulin de la Galette, depicting couples twirling in a sun-dappled Montmartre guinguette – you can almost hear the laughter and feel the love in that joyful scene. There's also Gustave Courbet's The Origin of the World... which, while extremely intimate (to put it mildly), underscores that love and attraction are timeless subjects. Perhaps the most literally romantic spot in Orsay is behind the giant transparent clock on the fifth floor. From inside, couples stand in the hollow of the clock face and gaze out at the panorama of Paris – it's an iconic photo spot and has a dreamy "time stands still" quality. In quiet corners, you might find a Rodin sculpture of a tender embrace, or a wistful painting of lovers parting at a train station (fitting for the former Gare d'Orsay). The building itself, with its grand arching roof, inspires a certain awe – it's not unusual to see someone spontaneously dip their partner for a kiss in the airy central hall (especially if a musician is playing the piano installed there). As you exit, perhaps at twilight, the Seine just outside and the glow of the city make for a continuation of the art-induced romance. If the Louvre is for intellectual stimulation, Orsay – with its Monets and Manets and moody Van Goghs – is for feeding the soul, preferably two souls in love.

Musée de Montmartre & Renoir Gardens (Museum) – Montmartre has long been a neighborhood of love – artistic love, bohemian love, and the sort of free love that had prudish Parisians clutching their pearls in the early 1900s. At the Musée de Montmartre, set in one of the oldest houses on the hill, you can soak in that rich artistic romance. This museum was once home to painter Pierre- Auguste Renoir (he painted Bal du Moulin de la Galette in its garden) and later a hangout for the young artists of the early 20th century. Its exhibits showcase the neighborhood's raucous cabaret history (yes, you'll see artifacts from the Chat Noir and the Lapin Agile, where many a fling surely started over absinthe) and the lives of artists like Suzanne Valadon, a talented painter who lived on site and whose love life was as colorful as her canvases. Step out into the Renoir Gardens behind the museum, and you'll find a quiet, lovely nook complete with swings, rose bushes, and a view of Montmartre's vineyard below. It's unexpectedly peaceful – you might hear the distant bells of Sacré- Cœur or the chatter from a nearby café, but mostly it's just you, your sweetheart, and maybe a wandering cat.

There's even a quaint café overlooking the greenery, perfect for a coffee or glass of wine to toast Montmartre's muse. Perhaps the spirit of Valadon and her lovers, or Renoir and his models, will sprinkle a bit of amour fou (crazy love) into your day. At the very least, you'll leave understanding why so many artists fell in love – with Montmartre, and with each other – in this little village on a hill.

Père Lachaise Cemetery (Cemetery) – It might sound morbid to list a cemetery in a romance guide, but Père Lachaise is no ordinary cemetery. This vast necropolis is one of the most beautiful and storied in the world, and among its winding paths lie the graves of lovers and poets who loved deeply. The most famous romantic tale here is that of Héloïse and Abélard, the star-crossed medieval lovers. Abélard was a philosopher who fell in love with his student Héloïse in the 12th century; their passionate affair led to secret marriage and tragic consequences (let's just say Abélard's guardians took extreme measures to ensure he'd join a monastery...). Separated in life, they were reunited in death – their remains rest together in an elaborate tomb at Père Lachaise. Today, their shared tomb is a pilgrimage site for lovers, who leave letters and flowers, moved by a romance that withstood scandal and the strictures of their time. Elsewhere, you'll find the grave of Oscar Wilde, once covered in lipstick kisses by admirers (a glass barrier now prevents direct smooching of the stone), or that of Édith Piaf, whose songs of love gained new poignancy after her own tumultuous relationships (including with boxer Marcel Cerdan, also buried here). As you and your partner wander the leafy avenues, hand in hand, you may find it oddly serene and reflective rather than spooky. Many of the monuments are themselves beautiful works of art – weeping angels, clasped hands, and affirmations of undying love carved in stone. It's said that a couple who kisses near the tomb of journalist Victor Noir (famous for the life-sized bronze statue on his grave, which is ahem rather anatomically emphasized for fertility legend) will have happiness forever. Whether or not that's true, Père Lachaise offers a quiet pause in your Paris explorations – a reminder that love can be everlasting, and that life is precious. It might just inspire you to hold each other a little closer.

Palais Garnier (Opera House) – Dripping in gilded glamour and topped with a phantom or two, the Palais Garnier is Paris's iconic 19th-century opera house – a temple to the arts that is inherently romantic. Stepping into its grand foyer and marble staircase is enough to make anyone feel like royalty on a night at the ball. Couples visiting by day can tour its opulent halls and maybe sneak into a plush red box to steal a kiss, channeling the famous Phantom of the Opera lore (Gaston Leroux's novel was set here, after all). Speaking of phantoms, the story of the disfigured musician hopelessly in love with the beautiful soprano Christine has tugged at heartstrings for over a century – and some say a visit to the Palais Garnier isn't complete without descending to peer at the underground lake that inspired that tale. The auditorium itself, with Marc Chagall's dreamy ceiling painting and the colossal chandelier, is a vision – one imagines all the love affairs sparked in those velvet seats, under cover of darkness and Tchaikovsky. By night, attending a ballet or opera here can be an incredibly romantic experience; you dress up, you sip champagne at intermission in the Belle Époque salon, you share glances that say: "we are really here, pinch me." In 1858, when Napoleon III's Empress Eugénie first saw the architect's designs for the opera, she reportedly asked if it would be in Greek or Roman style. "It's Napoleon III style, Madame," he replied cheekily. That blend of extravagance and confidence defines the Palais Garnier – it's extra, it's fabulous, and it's the perfect stage for your own love story, even if just for a day. (Bonus: outside, on the opera steps, is where many a young Parisian couple meets "à l'Opéra" as a central rendezvous point. Who knows, you might witness a first date awkwardly blossoming into something more, right in front of those golden lyres and masks.)

Place des Vosges & Maison de Victor Hugo (Square & Museum) – Place des Vosges is often hailed as Paris's most beautiful square – and who are we to argue? This perfectly symmetrically planned 17th-century square in Le Marais, with its red-brick arcaded buildings and a manicured central park, has an undeniable air of romance. Cardinal Richelieu, Madame de Sévigné, Colette – many famous figures lived around these elegant façades. But one resident in particular gives the square its romantic-literary pedigree: Victor Hugo. The great novelist and poet resided at No. 6 Place des Vosges (then called Place Royale) for 16 years. His apartment is now a museum – step inside, and you can almost sense the creative fervor; these walls bore witness to Hugo's passionate affairs. Most notably, Hugo carried on a lifelong romance with Juliette Drouet, an actress who gave up her career to devote herself to him and famously wrote him thousands of love letters. One can imagine Juliette visiting Hugo here in secret, walking under these very arcades perhaps, or Hugo gazing out at the square's central fountain, penning lines of love and revolution. Today, couples lounge on the grass or kiss on the benches in that little park, as children play and fountains murmur – it's idyllic. Grab some macarons from a nearby pâtisserie and have a mini picnic à deux. As you sit there, recall that this square also saw royal jousting matches and was a fashionable promenade for nobility – basically a

17th-century dating hotspot! In *Les Misérables*, Hugo wrote, "To love or have loved, that is enough." Standing in the Place des Vosges, with its timeless beauty and the spirit of Hugo in the air, you feel the truth of those words. It's a place that has seen centuries of love, survived upheavals, and remains as enchanting as ever – much like love itself.

Panoramic Paris: Views to Take Your Breath Away

Ascend to the city's most breathtaking viewpoints and iconic landmarks. Whether it's sharing a kiss atop the Eiffel Tower (where proposals happen almost daily) or watching the city lights twinkle from the steps of Sacré-Cœur, this chapter covers high-altitude romance with a dash of lighthearted commentary on the lengths (and heights) we go to for love.

Eiffel Tower (Tower) – Ah, La Tour Eiffel – arguably the world's most iconic symbol of love. This iron lattice tower, once decried as a monstrosity, has become the place where hearts flutter and knees bend (in proposals, that is). Standing 330 meters tall, she offers sweeping views of the city from three levels. By day, the vista is splendid, by night, absolutely magical as Paris sparkles below. Every year, countless couples ascend, and at least one ring gets presented with shaky hands and teary eyes, among the clouds. It's said proposals happen here nearly every day – no surprise, given the setting. The Eiffel Tower wasn't initially meant as a romantic symbol (it was an engineering marvel for the 1889 World's Fair), but over time it accrued so much romantic lore that now one can't separate Paris and romance from this structure. Perhaps it started in 1925 when pilot Pierre Labric clandestinely flew a plane between its legs for love (okay, that was more daredevil than romantic, but still). Or maybe when countless films like *An Affair to Remember* and *Midnight in Paris* cemented it as a backdrop for love. Fun fact: there was even a woman who "married" the Eiffel Tower in 2007 (truly – she's an objectophile named Erika who felt the Tower reciprocated her love; it was mentioned in a quirky tour guide). While that's, let's say, exceptional, it underscores the tower's charisma. For you and your partner, whether you choose to go up or simply bask in its presence from the Trocadéro across the river, the Eiffel Tower is bound to cast its spell. When it twinkles for five minutes on the hour after dark, don't be surprised if you feel a sudden urge to kiss – it's practically reflexive. Engineering may have built it, but love made it legendary.

Sacré-Cœur Basilica & Montmartre View (Hilltop Basilica) – Perched atop Montmartre, the highest hill in Paris, the white-domed Sacré-Cœur Basilica offers a vantage point that rivals the Eiffel Tower – and with a very different vibe. Whereas the Eiffel Tower is modern and glitzy, Sacré-Cœur is old-world and soulful. The climb up its steps (or the funicular ride, if you're saving energy) is rewarded by a breathtaking panorama of Paris sprawled below. It's especially popular at sunset, when the sky often blushes pink, making the city look like a living watercolor. The atmosphere on the basilica's steps is festive and bohemian: you might find street musicians strumming romantic ballads or local artists sketching the skyline. In the movie *Amélie*, it's in Montmartre that whimsical romance unfolds – indeed, if you wander a bit around the basilica, you might recognize the spot where Amélie leads Nino on a quirky treasure hunt. Many couples simply sit on those famous steps, shoulder to shoulder, sharing a crêpe or a bottle of wine, watching the City of Light twinkle on as day turns to night. It's said in a travel tip that "the ambiance on the steps in front of Sacré-Cœur, with a view over Paris, can make for a very romantic setting" – a bit of an understatement once you're actually there, witnessing it. The basilica itself, dedicated in 1919, was built as a symbol of peace – perhaps that's why an aura of serenity envelops the area despite the crowds. Step inside and you might catch hushed prayers or a choir's notes echoing – it can be moving, even for the non-religious. And if you're up for it, climb the dome together (300 steps) for an even higher perspective – overcoming that mini challenge as a duo, only to be greeted by a 360-degree view, gives a tiny sense of conquering the world together. Down in the square below, Place du Tertre, artists will draw your caricature as a loved-up couple if you like (cheesy but fun!). All in all, Montmartre's summit combines the thrill of heights, the charm of a village, and the sanctity of a basilica – a potent mix to elevate the heart.

Arc de Triomphe (Monument & Viewpoint) – Commissioned by Napoleon to celebrate his Grande Armée, the Arc de Triomphe is a monument to victories – but it can also be a monument to your personal victory in love (or at least a darn good Instagram shot together). Ascend the 284 steps to the top (or cheat with the elevator most of the way – we won't tell) and you'll find yourself at the center of a starburst of avenues, with Paris stretching in all directions. The view down the Champs- Élysées toward the Concorde and Louvre is iconic, but equally impressive is the line east to La Défense's modern arch, or north to Sacré-Cœur peeking out on its hill. This vantage point especially shines at night – many overlook that you can visit after dark – when the Champs-Élysées glitters with car lights like a stream of diamonds, and the Eiffel Tower sparkles at the hour behind you. It's less crowded up here than the Tower, giving couples a chance to find a quieter corner along the parapet to soak it all in. Perhaps you'll steal a kiss with the city lights as witnesses. Down below, the Arc is home to the Tomb of the Unknown Soldier, whose eternal flame is quite poetic – a symbol of memory and undying honor; some compare it to the eternal flame of love that must be kept burning (at least, a poet in your group might). Fun to note: Twelve avenues radiate from the Arc in a circle – called L'Étoile (the star) –

suggesting that from love's perspective, all paths in Paris lead back to a romantic moment at the Arc de Triomphe. And if you time it for Bastille Day (July 14) or New Year's, the Arc becomes the centerpiece of spectacular fireworks or light shows – truly triumphant backdrops for love. Standing above the city bustle, with the wind in your hair and your loved one by your side, you'll feel on top of the (Parisian) world.

Montparnasse Tower (Observation Deck) – Paris's skyline is famously low and lovely – except for the somewhat controversial Montparnasse Tower, a 210-meter modern skyscraper. The joke goes: the best thing about the view from Montparnasse's observation deck is that it's the only place in Paris where you can't see the Montparnasse Tower itself. Snarks aside, it's a phenomenal view, and indeed many prefer it to the Eiffel Tower's because here, you see the Eiffel Tower in all its glory as part of the panorama. The 56th-floor indoor observatory and the open-air roof terrace above provide a 360-degree vista. Going up around twilight is ideal: you watch the city turn golden, then blue, then light up dot by dot. A glass of champagne is on offer at the top – pricey, yes, but what's a toast at 200 meters high worth? There's even a Champagne bar on the roof in summer. Fewer tourists think to come here, so couples often have ample space to canoodle along the railing, pointing out landmarks to each other: "Look, there's Notre-Dame's buttresses, there's the golden dome of Invalides, oh and see that – that's where we had our first picnic!" On clear days you can see nearly 40 km away, which means you could metaphorically "see our future from up here," if one were inclined to wax poetic. Montparnasse Tower itself, despite being a dull office building, has a romantic surprise at ground level – the Ciel de Paris restaurant on the 56th floor, which for years held the title of the highest panoramic restaurant in town. Dining there as the sun sets is an experience of clinking glasses amidst clouds. One might initially think a modern tower doesn't fit in a historical romance guide, but love in Paris isn't stuck in the past – it reaches for the sky, just like this tower. And frankly, who can resist a view that makes the whole City of Love your backdrop? It's proposal-ready, should you need it, with the Eiffel's beacon literally shining a spotlight on your big moment.

Printemps Rooftop Terrace (Panoramic Café) – For a more casual but no less stunning vista, the rooftop of the Printemps department store offers a hidden-in-plain-sight gem. After navigating through perfumes and fashion on your way up (which could in itself become a flirtatious shopping date), you'll reach Le Déli-Cieux, the aptly named terrace café atop Printemps Haussmann. "Déli cieux" is a pun in French, sounding like "delicious" and meaning "from the skies" – and indeed, this view feels like a treat from the heavens. You get a front-row look at the ornate teal dome of Printemps next door, a sweeping outlook on the Opera Garnier's chimeras, and in the distance, the Eiffel Tower, Montmartre, and beyond. Since it's a café, you can grab a coffee or a light lunch and sit at a little table, clinking cups instead of champagne flutes, but the romantic effect is surprisingly similar. It's often less crowded than other viewpoints and free to access (just ride the elevator to the 8th or 9th floor of Printemps Maison). Many locals and in-the-know travelers bring their date here to impress without breaking the bank. There's something inherently sweet about sharing a city view over a simple coffee, perhaps splitting a pastry, and feeling a bit like you discovered a secret together. If the wind's brisk, cuddle up; if the sun's shining, share those sunglasses for a goofy pic with Paris at your feet. While not as famous as other vantage points, the Printemps terrace has seen its share of anniversaries celebrated and even a surprise proposal or two. It proves that in Paris, even a shopping trip can serendipitously turn into a scene from a rom-com, complete with panoramic cutaway.

Evening Enchantments: Paris After Dark

Experience the city's nocturnal charm with romantic nighttime activities. From moonlit Seine cruises to dancing cheek-to-cheek by the river, and classic cabaret shows, this chapter shows that Paris after dusk is a stage set for romance, complete with glittering lights, music wafting through the air, and maybe a ghost of a champagne-fueled poet or two.

Seine River Dinner Cruise (River Cruise Experience) – Drifting down the Seine on a Bateaux-Mouches or other dinner cruise is the stuff of Parisian fantasy. As night falls, you board a glass-enclosed boat, are shown to a private table, and as you clink champagne flutes, the illuminated Louvre glides by on one side and the golden dome of Les Invalides on the other. An evening cruise with a gourmet meal and live music is often touted as "the ideal way to end a romantic day," and indeed it's like floating through an Impressionist painting of Paris at night. The city's landmarks twinkle – Notre-Dame's buttresses lit up, Orsay's clock glowing – and then, highlight of highlights, the Eiffel Tower comes into view and bursts into its 20,000-bulb sparkle show, reflected in the river's surface. Many a heart has melted in that very moment. Some boats even pause near the tower to let everyone take it in (and probably to allow a few more rings to be presented across the dining room). The gentle lapping of water and soft French chansons, played by a live pianist or violinist, complete the ambiance. If you step onto the open deck after your main course, you'll feel the breeze and see Paris's bridges arching romantically overhead, each with its own story – Pont Marie with its kissing tradition, Pont des Arts with its now lock-free ironwork still bearing the memory of a million vows. There's an intimacy to being on a boat – perhaps it's the slight sway or the way you're cocooned from the city's noise – that makes you feel like the only two people in the world, even if other diners are around. Sure, it can be touristy, but cynicism melts away with the first sight of Notre-Dame's towers lit like a beacon or the second sip of bubbly. As you disembark into the night, hand in hand, you might find yourself humming "La Vie en Rose" along with the accordion that played during dessert, fully convinced that Paris is, in fact, a moveable feast of love.

Quais de Seine Tango (Seine-Side Dance Spot) – On warm evenings, something magical happens along the Seine's quays near the Jardin Tino Rossi (by the Institut du Monde Arabe). Locals and visitors alike gather at the riverside amphitheaters to dance tango under the open sky. It's informal, it's free, and it's very sexy in that understated French way. Around sunset, someone sets up a speaker, the nostalgic strains of Argentine tango begin, and couples – from spry youths to silver- haired enthusiasts – embrace and start gliding over the concrete as if it were a polished dance floor. Even if you don't dance, it's a treat to watch. As one guide notes, "local tango dancers gather to dance by the Seine... Even if you don't know how to dance tango, it's very nice to sit and watch on a summer evening, and quite romantic!" Indeed, spectators often end up swaying on the sidelines or nudging their partner to take a spin. If you two are brave, a friendly dancer might show you a few basic steps – or just hold each other close and do your own slow shuffle; no one minds. The backdrop is killer: Notre-Dame upstream, the Île Saint-Louis lights reflecting in the water, boats cruising by with their own music which sometimes cheekily competes with the tango rhythms. There's a communal feeling of joy; strangers dance together, yet there's also space for intimate connection – each dance is like a little three-minute love affair. If tango isn't on, sometimes there's salsa or swing depending on the night, but tango is the classic. We'd argue there are few things more romantic than a spontaneous dance with your love under the Parisian moon, with the Seine as your witness. It's the kind of moment where you think, "Is this real life? Are we in a movie?" And then you dip your partner (or attempt to) and laughter assures you it's delightfully real.

Moulin Rouge Cabaret (Night Show) – The Moulin Rouge is flamboyant, kitschy, touristy – and yet, there's no denying its iconic status as a place where romance and wild entertainment meet. This Belle Époque cabaret in Montmartre, with its famous red windmill on top, was the birthplace of the can-can and the bohemian fin-de-siècle nightlife immortalized by Toulouse-Lautrec's posters. Going to a show here is like stepping into a Technicolor dream of feathers, sequins, and exuberant dancing. Couples often make a whole glamorous date of it: dressing up, popping champagne at a tiny table, and watching the elaborate revue unfold. There's something inherently romantic about sharing a bit of cheeky fun – you'll exchange amused glances as performers high-kick in unison or a daring acrobat act makes everyone gasp. The Moulin Rouge's show changes theme periodically, but it is always a spectacle of fantastical sets and costumes. While it's not "romantic" in the traditional candlelight-and-roses sense, it's the kind of over-the-top experience that creates a giddy shared memory. And perhaps surprisingly, the Moulin Rouge has its tender side: interspersed with all the bawdy razzle-dazzle, there might be a solo ballerina or a moving musical segment that momentarily stills the crowd, and you find your partner squeezing your hand in the dark. Historically, the cabaret has seen its share of famous romances – from star dancers wooed by princes to artistes falling for their muses. And of course, it inspired the modern film Moulin Rouge! – a tragic love story that had everyone sobbing into their popcorn. Fear not, attending the real Moulin Rouge is usually far more joyful. As you leave, Montmartre's Pigalle area will be buzzing, but you two can wander up the hill a bit to see the city lights below, letting the evening air cool your flushed cheeks. The slogan goes, "The show must go on," and in Paris, so must the love.

Midnight Stroll on Pont Alexandre III (Bridge at Night) – We started our journey with Seine-side strolls, but it's worth ending with one too, for the atmosphere is entirely transformed by night. Picture this: it's past 11 p.m., dinner is done, and the city's hustle quiets to a murmur. You and your beloved find yourselves drawn to Pont Alexandre III once more. The bridge's ornate lamps are lit, casting a soft glow on the gilded statues that guard it. The Seine reflects all the lights, quivering like a million little stars. Perhaps you hear distant laughter from a party boat, or the flutter of a night bird. Walking in the center of this bridge at midnight, you feel like you own Paris. In the distance, the Eiffel Tower beams its searchlight, as if knowingly sweeping over to check on you two. Filmmakers have chosen this very spot as the quintessential romantic rendezvous – remember in *Midnight in Paris*, where Gil meets Gabrielle as it rains? That was here, and indeed if a little drizzle catches you, don't even fret – it only adds to the cinematic romance (just maybe protect any silk dresses!). You lean on the railing together, perhaps quietly humming "Sous le Ciel de Paris" (Under Paris Skies), watching the water. Bridges have a symbolic weight – they connect two sides, much like love connects two souls. And Pont Alexandre III, being arguably the most beautiful, feels like a promise that the connection will be grand and enduring. In the stillness, maybe you'll whisper dreams for the future, or reminisce about the trip's highlights, or simply enjoy a comfortable silence. If you're lucky, you might have the bridge almost to yourselves save a lone photographer or a passing couple. In those moments, Paris feels like it's all yours – a private backdrop to your love. As you finally stroll away, arm around waist, you realize why Paris at night is called the City of Light – not just for the lamps and bulbs, but for how it lights up our hearts. Bon nuit, les amoureux (good night, lovers).

Honeymoon Hideaways: Romantic Hotels and Love Nests

Conclude with a selection of Paris's most charming places to stay for two. Lavish historic hotels that hosted famous lovers, chic boutique hideaways in artists' quarters, and even a hotel literally named "Amour" – this chapter ensures travelers end their day in a setting as romantic as the adventures that preceded. Expect a playful peek into sumptuous suites and maybe a wink at the things not found in the history books.

Hôtel Ritz Paris (Luxury Hotel) – The Ritz is not just a hotel; it's a legend in bricks and mortar (and gilding). Situated on the elegant Place Vendôme, the Ritz has been the backdrop for endless love stories since it opened in 1898. Coco Chanel lived here for decades (rumor has it she said, "The only real luxury is the luxury of human companionship," perhaps gazing from her Ritz suite onto the square below). F. Scott Fitzgerald and Zelda caroused in its halls during the Jazz Age, and Hemingway famously "liberated" the Ritz bar after WWII, later writing, "When I dream of afterlife in heaven, the action always takes place at the Hôtel Ritz Paris." With its sumptuous Louis XVI décor, the Ritz feels like a royal palace, and checking in as a couple can make you feel like king and queen – or movie stars. In fact, many a film has tried to capture its aura (think *Love in the Afternoon* with Audrey Hepburn). The suites are named after romantic luminaries – imagine staying in the Windsor Suite, named after the Duke and Duchess of Windsor, who romanced here, or the Imperial Suite, which is a national monument in itself for its opulence. If a stay is beyond budget, a cocktail at the Ritz's Hemingway Bar or a pastry at the Vendôme Bar terrace can still let you bask in the atmosphere.

Proposals frequently happen under the crystal chandeliers of its Michelin-star restaurant or in its private garden with tinkling fountain. Even a stroll through its lobby can evoke sighs – you might spot a bride in couture having a photoshoot on the grand staircase. The phrase "meet me at the Ritz" has long meant "let's have a clandestine rendezvous in luxury." Indeed, the Ritz has discretion down to an art (one reason so many famous lovers from royalty to Hollywood choose it). If walls could talk, the Ritz's would whisper tales of midnight champagne toasts, of forbidden kisses behind pillar mirrors, of love rekindled over tea in the Salon Proust. And when you snuggle into its famously cloud-like beds, you might just find yourself saying what many have said upon departure: "Darling, when we return to Paris, let's do exactly this again."

Hôtel Plaza Athénée (Luxury Hotel) – With its signature red awnings and geranium-bedecked balconies, the Plaza Athénée on Avenue Montaigne is the picture of Parisian romance. This is where Carrie Bradshaw stayed in the final season of Sex and the City, awaiting her Mr. Big – and indeed the views of the Eiffel Tower from some suites here could make anyone swoon. Since 1913, the Plaza has welcomed amorous guests including Grace Kelly, Elizabeth Taylor (multiple honeymoons!), and a roster of who's-who in love. What sets it apart is a blend of glam and warmth: the Art Deco meets Louis XVI interiors are gorgeous without being intimidating. Couples often celebrate anniversaries here – imagine a private dinner on your balcony with the Eiffel Tower sparkling every hour, or descending to the courtyard restaurant where, under fairy lights and with impeccable service, you feel like you're in a modern fairytale. One of the Plaza's restaurants is even called the "Cour Jardin" – a courtyard that in winter turns into an ice-skating rink; yes, you can skate hand-in-hand in a couture courtyard, how dreamy (and somewhat surreal). The staff have seen it all: they can help arrange rose petals in your room, surprise proposals, or simply ensure your breakfast in bed comes with a side of croissants shaped like hearts (okay, that's not on the menu, but the sentiment is there). The Avenue Montaigne location means you're steps from luxury boutiques – perhaps dangerous for the wallet, but a stroll here also offers spontaneous romantic fun (window-shopping Dior gowns and picking imaginary outfits for each other). The hotel's bar is a sultry spot too: order two of their famed "Rose Royale" cocktails (champagne with raspberry and rose) and toast to your love. By the time you depart the Plaza Athénée, don't be surprised if you've left a piece of your heart nestled among those red geraniums – or at least in the ultra-plush pillows with the embroidered initials "HPA" (which, in your mind, might stand for Happily Passionate Always).

Hôtel Particulier Montmartre (Boutique Hotel) – Tucked away in a secret alley of Montmartre, guarded by high walls and accessible through a tiny private gate, lies the aptly named Hôtel Particulier – a hidden mansion turned ultra-chic boutique hotel. With only five suites, it's one of the most exclusive and intimate stays in Paris. Each suite is uniquely designed by contemporary artists and designers – expect quirky, sensual luxury (one room has walls painted with exotic foliage and monkeys, another with subtle erotic sketches – it's definitely a place that encourages l'amour with a playful wink). The real seduction, however, is the setting: a lush private garden that feels worlds away from the city. You can have breakfast under the trees or cocktails at their chic bar Le Très Particulier, which is like a speakeasy in a conservatory, dripping with greenery and vintage glamour. This hotel was literally a love nest historically – the property once belonged to the Hermès family and is rumored to have hosted some artistic trysts. Montmartre being what it is, you're near the famous steps and the artistic squares, but here you get a haven of peace after the bohemian bustle. Imagine coming "home" to this sanctuary after a day of exploring: the path lit softly, the scent of jasmine in the air, and maybe a cat slinking by (Montmartre has its friendly felines). Because of its seclusion, many celebrities choose it for getaways, but it's equally perfect for any couple who values privacy and charm over big hotel pomp. Staying here feels like being let in on one of Paris's best-kept secrets – you're insiders in the Montmartre of old, where behind unassuming doors lay gardens of delight and clandestine romance. It's the kind of place where you might end up spending more time in your suite than out – and that's entirely by design.

Hotel Amour (Boutique Hotel) – The name says it all. Amour means love, and this trendy boutique hotel in the South Pigalle (SoPi) district fully embraces the theme with a cheeky, modern twist. Opened by a former fashion photographer and nightclub guru, Hotel Amour is all about style and sensuality. Each room is unique – decorated by different artists and designers – and some can be quite risqué (one has pin-up photos, another a round bed under a mirrored ceiling... oh la la!). But it's done in a hip, youthful way that feels fun rather than seedy. In fact, the whole neighborhood has transformed from the old red-light Pigalle days to a vibrant area of cocktail bars, bistros, and concept stores – often dubbed "the Nouvelle Athènes" for its artistic vibe. Downstairs, the hotel's café is a popular spot for brunch and late-night drinks, spilling into a patio filled with plants; many locals don't realize it's part of a hotel at all, it just feels like the place to be. Staying at Hotel Amour as a couple is like being admitted to the cool kids' club, one where romance is playful. The staff even sells their own line of Amour merchandise (like t-shirts and, fittingly, boxer shorts) – a souvenir of your amorous adventure. Don't expect phones or TVs in the rooms; the idea is to focus on ahem more interpersonal entertainment. Perhaps channel the ghosts of Pigalle's artistic past: could that be Pablo Picasso and his lover Fernande stepping out of that doorway, or Édith Piaf and a paramour giggling over a secret joke? The spirit of free love and creativity lingers here. While Hotel Amour isn't about over-the-top luxury, it offers something arguably better for young (or young-at-heart) lovers: a place where you can be a bit naughty, a bit carefree, and very much in love, all with Paris's coolest crowd just outside your door.

Pavillon de la Reine (Luxury Boutique Hotel) – Tucked under the arcades of the regal Place des Vosges, the Pavillon de la Reine is a hotel fit for royalty – literally named "Queen's Pavilion" after Queen Anne of Austria, who once lived in the square. Discreet ivy-covered entrances lead into a world of refined elegance. If you fantasize about living in a Parisian mansion with courtyards and antique furnishings, this is your spot. The hotel combines historic charm (wood-beamed ceilings, oil paintings, period furniture) with modern comforts and an indulgent spa. Many rooms have canopied beds and deep-soaking tubs – ideal for a romantic retreat after wandering the Marais. Despite its location on the popular Place des Vosges, the hotel is whisper-quiet, especially in its flowered courtyard where you can take breakfast or afternoon tea as if in a private castle garden. What could be more romantic than sipping champagne there at twilight, the arcade's lamps casting a warm glow on the cobblestones, a harp perhaps playing softly through an open window (hey, it could happen)? The hotel's ambiance evokes centuries past, but it's very much attuned to the needs of contemporary lovebirds – staff can arrange private museum tours or horse-drawn carriage rides if you desire. Because it sits in Paris's oldest planned square, you're steeped in history: Victor Hugo's house is a few doors down (where he wrote love letters upstairs), and Madame de Sévigné penned her famous correspondence nearby. But step outside, and you'll also find trendy art galleries and cafes at your feet. This mix of old and new makes Pavillon de la Reine special. It's the sort of place where a proposal in the courtyard feels naturally in tune with the surroundings (we wouldn't be surprised if a few have taken place by the trickling fountain). The Marais means "swamp" originally, but fear not – the only thing you might be sinking into here is a plush four-poster bed after a day of Marais adventures, whispering bonne nuit as the echoes of this storied quarter lull you to sleep. In the morning, wake up and look out at Place des Vosges before the world arrives – it'll feel like Paris put on a show just for the two of you.

Each location above offers its own blend of historical context and modern charm, proving that in Paris, romance is woven into every cobblestone and café chair. Whether it's the grand gesture of a proposal atop the Eiffel Tower or the quiet thrill of discovering a secret courtyard together, the city provides an endless stage for love – often with a knowing wink and a dash of humor. After all, this is the city that has inspired poets to rhyme, painters to swoon, and even the most seasoned travelers to believe in a bit of everyday magic. Paris loves lovers, and as both newcomers and seasoned visitors will find, its mix of well- known icons and hidden gems ensures that love here is always an adventure, steeped in history, wrapped in beauty, and finished with a gentle laugh or two – the perfect recipe for memories that, like a fine French wine, only grow sweeter with time.

Complete List of 60 Romantic Spots in Paris –
Sorted by Arrondissement

Place	Address	Closest Metro	Arrondissement
Jardin du Palais Royal	43 Rue de Valois, 75001 Paris	Palais Royal – Musée du Louvre	1st
Place Dauphine	Place Dauphine, 75001 Paris	Pont Neuf	1st
Place Vendôme	Place Vendôme, 75001 Paris	Opéra	1st
Pont Neuf	Pont Neuf, 75001 Paris	Pont Neuf	1st
Pont des Arts	Pont des Arts, 75001 Paris	Louvre – Rivoli	1st
Square du Vert-Galant	1 Square du Vert Galant, 75001 Paris	Pont Neuf	1st
Square du Vert-Galant	1 Square du Vert Galant, 75001 Paris	Pont Neuf	1st
Galerie Vivienne	4 Rue des Petits Champs, 75002 Paris	Bourse	2nd
Rue Montorgueil	Rue Montorgueil, 75002 Paris	Sentier	2nd

Jardin Anne-Frank	14 Impasse Berthaud, 75003 Paris	Rambuteau	3rd
Square Saint-Gilles-du-Grand-Veneur	Rue de Hesse, 75003 Paris	Chemin Vert	3rd
Square du Temple – Elie Wiesel	64 Rue de Bretagne, 75003 Paris	Temple	3rd
Au Vieux Paris d'Arcole	24 Rue Chanoinesse, 75004 Paris	Cité	4th
Hôtel de Sully Garden	62 Rue Saint-Antoine, 75004 Paris	Saint-Paul	4th
Jardin des Rosiers – Joseph-Migneret	10 Rue des Rosiers, 75004 Paris	Saint-Paul	4th
Place des Vosges	Place des Vosges, 75004 Paris	Chemin Vert	4th
Pont Marie	Pont Marie, 75004 Paris	Pont Marie	4th
Rue des Barres	Rue des Barres, 75004 Paris	Pont Marie	4th
Square Jean XXIII	4 Parvis Notre-Dame, 75004 Paris	Cité	4th

Village Saint-Paul	Rue Saint-Paul, 75004 Paris	Saint-Paul	4th
Île Saint-Louis & Place Louis Aragon	Quai de Bourbon, 75004 Paris	Pont Marie	4th
Jardin des Plantes	57 Rue Cuvier, 75005 Paris	Gare d'Austerlitz	5th
Rue Mouffetard	Rue Mouffetard, 75005 Paris	Place Monge	5th
Saint-Étienne-du-Mont	Place Sainte-Geneviève, 75005 Paris	Cardinal Lemoine	5th
Square René-Viviani	25 Quai de Montebello, 75005 Paris	Saint-Michel	5th
Jardin du Luxembourg	Rue de Médicis – Rue de Vaugirard, 75006 Paris	Luxembourg	6th
Place de Furstenberg	Place de Furstenberg, 75006 Paris	Saint-Germain-des-Prés	6th
Jardin du Musée Rodin	77 Rue de Varenne, 75007 Paris	Varenne	7th
Promenade des Berges de Seine	Port de Solférino, 75007 Paris	Assemblée Nationale	7th

Rue Saint-Dominique	Rue Saint-Dominique, 75007 Paris	École Militaire	7th
Musée Jacquemart-André	158 Boulevard Haussmann, 75008 Paris	Miromesnil	8th
Parc Monceau	35 Boulevard de Courcelles, 75008 Paris	Monceau	8th
Pont Alexandre III	Pont Alexandre III, 75008 Paris	Invalides	8th
Musée de la Vie Romantique	16 Rue Chaptal, 75009 Paris	Pigalle	9th
Musée de la Vie Romantique Garden Café	16 Rue Chaptal, 75009 Paris	Pigalle	9th
Place Saint-Georges	Place Saint-Georges, 75009 Paris	Saint-Georges	9th
Square Édouard VII	Square Édouard VII, 75009 Paris	Opéra	9th
Canal Saint-Martin	Quai de Valmy, 75010 Paris	République	10th
Bois de Vincennes	Route de la Pyramide, 75012 Paris	Château de Vincennes	12th

Parc Floral de Paris	Route de la Pyramide, 75012 Paris	Château de Vincennes	12th
Promenade Plantée	1 Coulée verte René-Dumont, 75012 Paris	Bastille	12th
Rue Crémieux	Rue Crémieux, 75012 Paris	Gare de Lyon	12th
Square des Peupliers	Square des Peupliers, 75013 Paris	Tolbiac	13th
Parc Montsouris	2 Rue Gazan, 75014 Paris	Cité Universitaire	14th
Parc André Citroën	2 Rue Cauchy, 75015 Paris	Balard	15th
Parc Georges Brassens	2 Place Jacques Marette, 75015 Paris	Convention	15th
Petite Ceinture Trail	Entrée: 26 Rue de l'Avre, 75015 Paris	La Motte-Picquet – Grenelle	15th
Pont de Bir-Hakeim	Pont de Bir-Hakeim, 75015 Paris	Bir-Hakeim	15th
Parc de Bagatelle	Bois de Boulogne, Route de Sèvres à Neuilly, 75016 Paris	Pont de Neuilly (plus a walk or bus)	16th

Square des Batignolles	144bis Rue Cardinet, 75017 Paris	Brochant	17th
Hôtel Particulier Montmartre	23 Avenue Junot, 75018 Paris	Lamarck–Caulaincourt	18th
La Maison Rose	2 Rue de l'Abreuvoir, 75018 Paris	Lamarck–Caulaincourt	18th
Montmartre Vineyards	14–18 Rue des Saules, 75018 Paris	Lamarck–Caulaincourt	18th
Place des Abbesses	Place des Abbesses, 75018 Paris	Abbesses	18th
Rue Lepic	Rue Lepic, 75018 Paris	Abbesses	18th
Square Louise Michel	6 Place Saint-Pierre, 75018 Paris	Abbesses	18th
Square Marcel Bleustein-Blanchet	Rue de la Bonne, 75018 Paris	Abbesses	18th
Parc de la Villette	211 Avenue Jean Jaurès, 75019 Paris	Porte de Pantin	19th
Parc des Buttes-Chaumont	1 Rue Botzaris, 75019 Paris	Buttes-Chaumont	19th

Parc de Belleville	47 Rue des Couronnes, 75020 Paris	Couronnes	20th

Part II:
Parisian Quirks &
Historical Lore

If you love unusual history and eyebrow-raising facts, you'll love this section. These 50 quirky tales and hidden historical gems take you through odd laws, scandalous secrets, strange inventions, and surprising turns in Paris's past. Warning: your dinner party storytelling skills are about to level up.

Offbeat, Oddball, and Oh-So-Parisian

Let's face it—Paris has a wonderfully weird side. Beyond the glimmer of chandeliers and carefully choreographed romance, the city hides centuries of mischief, mystery, and magnificent oddities. This section is your passport to the peculiar.

You'll wander into chapels built by mistresses, marvel at mummified relics in tucked-away museums, and hear the whispers of Revolution-era schemes still echoing in cobblestone courtyards. Some stories might make you laugh out loud (yes, we're looking at you, taxidermized rats in military uniforms), while others will have you scratching your head and wondering, "How is this not more famous?"

What to Expect

These 50 tales take you off the beaten route (pun fully intended) and sometimes on a well-worn path with lesser-known stories attached, into lesser-known neighborhoods, overlooked corners of famous landmarks, and even a few places you'll pass by three times before spotting the plaque. But each one reveals something unexpected— about Paris, about history, and maybe even about how delightfully human we all are.

Some are real (scandalously so), others are steeped in myth or legend. All are memorable.

How to Use This Section

Perfect for the endlessly curious, the history nerd, or the traveler who's already "done" Paris and wants a new adventure. Read it like a treasure hunt or sprinkle these stops into your itinerary as palate cleansers between museums and macaron shops.

Paris has always been a city of layers. This one's for the layer that wears a monocle, sips absinthe, and once challenged a pigeon to a duel. (Probably.)

* All addresses are documented and organized (by arrondissement, including metro stops) at the end of this section.

Off the Beaten Rue: 50 Weird and Wonderful Tales of Paris

Rue Chanoinesse (Île de la Cité) – Sweeney Todd of Paris (Medieval Legend) – Tucked behind Notre-Dame, this quiet street once "hosted" a 14th-century horror legend. A barber and a baker allegedly conspired to murder customers and bake them into meat pies for unwitting Parisians. The tale goes that a dog's frantic barking led authorities to discover the gruesome pâté fillings. Today at 20 Rue Chanoinesse (now a police station), you won't find man-eating pastries – just a plaque and perhaps a shiver if you know where to look.

Palais Garnier (Opéra House) – Phantom and the Underground Lake – The ornate opera house hides a subterranean secret: a water-filled chamber below the stage. This "lake" (actually a cistern) inspired the lair in The Phantom of the Opera. In 1896, a real chandelier counterweight fell and killed an audience member – an eerie plot point in Gaston Leroux's novel. Visitors can tour the opera. Staff even keep fish in the underground reservoir, proving that truth is stranger than fiction in these flamboyant halls.

Place Marcel-Aymé (Montmartre) – Le Passe-Muraille (Man Who Walked Through Walls) – In a tiny Montmartre square, a bronze man literally walks through a wall. This whimsical statue honors Marcel Aymé's 1943 story Le Passe-Muraille, about a mild-mannered clerk who discovers he can phase through walls – until he loses the power mid-stride. The poor fellow is frozen in the stone here, his hand polished shiny by countless people trying to "pull" him out. Rub his outstretched hand for luck, but be careful – you might end up stuck in Paris too!

***Notre-Dame Cathedral* – The Devil's Doorway (Biscornet's Wrought Iron)** – The medieval ironwork on Notre-Dame's side doors was so intricate that locals whispered the craftsman, Biscornet, must have had help from Satan. Legend says he sold his soul to forge the gorgeous scrolling patterns overnight. During the cathedral's opening, the doors initially refused to open until holy water was sprinkled, confirming diabolical involvement (or so the story goes). Next time you admire the wrought iron, remember the deals that might have been struck to create Paris's most famous hinges.

***Jardin des Tuileries* – The "Little Red Man" Ghost** – Amid the peaceful Tuileries Garden, keep an eye out for a short phantom in red. Catherine de Médicis' 16th-century soothsayer, a butcher nicknamed Jean l'Écorcheur was murdered and cursed the palace. Since then, this diminutive Red Man purportedly appeared to French royals and emperors as a harbinger of doom. He's said to have chatted with Napoléon himself in the emperor's heyday – only to vanish before Waterloo. The Tuileries Palace burned down in 1871, but the Red Man's legend lives on as a macabre Parisian omen.

***Le Procope (Latin Quarter)* –** Napoleon's Forgotten Hat (Historic Café) – Open since 1686, Paris's oldest café has hosted everyone from Voltaire to Benjamin Franklin. Its strangest heirloom? Napoleon Bonaparte's cocked hat, left here as an impoverished young officer. As the story goes, in 1795 the cash-strapped Napoleon pawned his iconic bicorne to pay for dinner – and never returned for it. The café proudly displays this hat to this day. Dine at Le Procope and you can see it under glass, a reminder that even future emperors might skip out on the bill!

12 Rue Chabanais (2nd Arr.) – Royal Brothel & Champagne Bathtub – This unassuming office building was once Le Chabanais, the most luxurious brothel of the Belle Époque. King Edward VII ("Dirty Bertie") was a regular and even installed a custom copper champagne-filled bathtub shaped like a sphinx for his frothy romps. Toulouse-Lautrec contributed erotic paintings to the theme rooms. When brothels were outlawed in 1946, Le Chabanais closed, and its lavish furniture was auctioned off. Today only a pair of now-stationary vintage elevators remain from this gilded pleasure palace – the stories, however, are still bubbling.

Paris Catacombs (Denfert-Rochereau) – Lost Man and Haunted Tunnels – The Catacombs house the bones of 6 million people in labyrinthine tunnels, but they're also home to spooky lore. One famous tale is of Philibert Aspairt, a doorkeeper who wandered into the catacombs in 1793 (looking for lost wine, says one version) and became hopelessly lost in the dark. His body was found 11 years later identified by the keys on his belt. Cataphiles (urban explorers) whisper that Philibert's ghost haunts the galleries every November 3, the anniversary of his disappearance. The catacombs' creepy vibe even inspired the horror film As Above, So Below – after midnight, some swear you can hear disembodied voices urging you to venture "deeper." Enter with caution (and a guide!) and stick to the official tour – lest you become the next lost soul in this empire of the dead.

Musée des Vampires (Les Lilas, just outside Paris) – A Vampire Scholar's Lair – Tucked in a garden shed on Paris's outskirts is a museum dedicated entirely to vampires and monstrosities. Eccentric scholar Jacques Sirgent created this by-appointment-only cabinet of curiosities, complete with a "vampire killing kit," mummified cats, and walls of Dracula posters. You enter through a black-and-scarlet gate into a faux graveyard strewn with (real!) human bones and plastic bats. Inside, Sirgent – a self-proclaimed vampirologist – will happily regale you with lore of medieval cults and "cannibal sorcery". It's equal parts educational and spooky fun. No worries, he doesn't bite... as long as you don't misbehave.

Théâtre du Grand-Guignol (Pigalle) – Horror Theater with Fainting Spells – In a tiny former chapel on Rue Chaptal, the Grand-Guignol theater staged such gore-fests from 1897 to 1962 that it reportedly caused two audience faintings a night. This theater specialized in naturalistic horror plays – think realistic stabbings, eyegouging, and spurting blood so shocking that patrons vomited or passed out. They even kept a house doctor on staff for the overwhelmed spectators! The phrase "grand guignol" became synonymous with grotesque drama. Today the building still stands (now a normal theater), but its legacy lives on in every slasher flick. Talk about bloody entertainment – perfect for date night, if your sweetheart doesn't mind a little scream.

Paris Sewers (Égouts Museum) – The 1984 Sewer Crocodile – No, it's not an urban myth – a live crocodile really was found swimming in the Paris sewers! On March 7, 1984, sewer workers under Pont Neuf spotted an 80 cm Nile crocodile lurking in a side tunnel. Firefighters captured the reptile, later nicknamed "Éléonore," which had likely been an ill-considered pet dumped when it got too big. After dining on Parisian rats for who knows how long, Éléonore was relocated to the Aquarium in Vannes, Brittany, where she grew into a 2.5 m adult living out her days in a replica sewer habitat. Visitors can tour the Paris Sewer Museum – and while you won't find any crocs now, you can see where this scaly legend made a splash in 1984.

Clos Montmartre (Montmartre) – The Hidden Urban Vineyard – High on Montmartre's hill, amid cabarets and cafes, lies a tiny working vineyard – a true grape-growing oddity in a metropolis. Clos Montmartre was planted in 1933 by local artists and residents to thwart developers who wanted to build over a Montmartre green space. (By French law, you can't dig up a vineyard – clever, non?) This mini vineyard produces a few hundred bottles of wine each year. The quality? Let's say it's more about the fun than the flavor. Every October the Fête des Vendanges brings a joyful harvest festival with parades and tastings. Visitors can peek at the vines from Rue des Saules, and while the wine itself might not win awards, the story behind it is intoxicating.

Père Lachaise Cemetery – The Fertility Grave of Victor Noir – Victor Noir was a 19-year-old journalist shot in 1870, now remembered less for politics than for his suggestive bronze tomb statue. The life-sized sculpture depicts Noir lying flat with a noticeable bulge in his pants, which (along with his dreamy face) has made him a posthumous sex symbol. According to legend, touching the statue's prominent protuberance or kissing Victor's lips grants enhanced fertility or a lover within the year. Generations of visitors (and hopeful would-be mothers) have done so – the effigy's lips and groin are polished shiny from all the rubbing. The trend became so... enthusiastic that authorities briefly fenced it off in 2004, only to face outraged protests. Today the barrier is gone. You can find Victor in Division 92 of Père Lachaise, his bronze anatomy gleaming and ready for your wishes (just keep it PG-13, please).

Place Dalida (Montmartre) – The Shiny-Bosomed Bust – Tucked in a leafy Montmartre square is a bronze bust of French chanteuse Dalida, a beloved 20th-century icon. Fans have adopted an... unusual ritual: for luck in love, one gently rubs the statue's breasts. As a result, Dalida's bust is literally busty and lustrous – its chest gleams bright gold compared to the weathered bronze elsewhere, thanks to countless caresses. No one's quite sure how this superstition started, but it fits a singer known for her passionate love songs. The square (named for Dalida, who lived nearby) offers one of Montmartre's prettiest views. Stop by, make a wish, and maybe Dalida's spirit will bless your amorous endeavors – her statue certainly isn't shy about lending a hand.

Flame of Liberty (Alma Bridge) – Unintentional Princess Diana Memorial – Erected in 1989 as a gilded replica of the Statue of Liberty's torch (a thank-you gift for restoring the Statue in NYC), this flame sculpture took on new meaning in 1997. It stands above the tunnel where Princess Diana tragically died, and grieving fans turned it into an impromptu Diana memorial – covering the base with flowers, notes, and graffiti. The monument itself was not meant to be tied to Diana at all, yet today many tourists assume it is her official memorial. The city has left it as-is, effectively allowing a "People's Shrine." By the way, the torch was originally a symbol of Franco-American friendship. Now it symbolizes the enduring public affection for "the People's Princess." Stop by Place de l'Alma day or night – the flame is always there, unofficially keeping Diana's memory alive.

Arago Medallions (All Over Paris) – The Other Paris Meridian – We all know about Greenwich, but did you know Paris once considered itself the Prime Meridian of the world? In fact, a bronze line of 135 Arago medallions sneaks through Paris's streets along the old Paris Meridian. These 12 cm bronze discs are embedded in sidewalks from north to south, each marked "ARAGO" (honoring the 19th-century astronomer François Arago) and labeled N and S. They form a 9 km trail – you can spot them near the Paris Observatory, across Luxembourg Garden, even by the Louvre. Dan Brown fans might recall the "Rose Line" in *The Da Vinci Code* – a fictionalized version of this. In reality, the Arago medallions were installed in 1994 as a quirky monument to France's once-proud zero longitude. Next time you "step on zero" at Notre-Dame's Point Zéro, consider hunting a few Arago markers too – a free treasure hunt in plain sight.

Square de l'Île-de-France (Ile de la Cité) – The Old Paris Morgue – This peaceful little park behind Notre-Dame hides a grisly past: it's the former site of the Paris Morgue, once the city's strangest public attraction. In the 19th century, unidentified corpses were displayed on marble slabs behind big glass windows here – literally a window-shopping spot for the morbidly curious. Parisians of all classes would stroll in to gawk at the latest bodies pulled from the Seine, often in various states of decomposition. At its peak, up to 40,000 people a day filed through the Morgue's "salle d'exposition" to glimpse death up close. This was considered both public service and free entertainment (Victorian values, huh). The Morgue was closed in 1907, but if you visit the park today you'll find a plaque noting its existence. Enjoy the lovely view of the Seine – and imagine the chilling scene here 150 years ago, when Parisians treated death like a day at the museum.

Arènes de Lutèce (5th Arr.) – A Roman Arena in Paris – Yes, Paris has a Roman gladiator arena – and it's hiding in plain sight in the

Latin Quarter! The Arènes de Lutèce, built in the 1st century AD, once seated 15,000 and hosted gladiatorial combats and wild animal fights. Over the centuries it was buried and forgotten. Fast forward to 1869: during Haussmann's renovations, workers rediscovered the ruins. A campaign led by writer Victor Hugo helped save it from destruction. Today it's a public park (accessible at 49 Rue Monge), where locals play football and pétanque on the ancient stage. You can still see the tiered stone seating and the outline of the arena floor. It's surreal – one minute you're in busy Paris, the next you're standing where gladiators roared "Ave Caesar!" Whether you're into history or just a unique picnic spot, this little amphitheater is an under-the-radar gem of Roman Lutetia.

Point Zéro des Routes de France (Notre-Dame Parvis) – The Center of France (and Kissing Spot) – Embedded in the cobblestones just outside Notre-Dame's front doors is a small bronze compass rose marking Point Zéro, the official center of Paris (and France's road distances). It's easy to miss – look down for a star-shaped disk about 20 cm wide. Tradition says standing on Point Zéro brings good luck, or ensures you'll return to Paris. Couples often hop on it to kiss (after all, you're literally at the heart of the City of Love). Others throw a coin on it for wishes. The spot is worn shiny by decades of feet and folklore. Next time you're at Notre-Dame, find the little star among the stones – you can literally say you've been at the absolute center of Paris. And if you spin around on it? Well, you're symbolically spinning around France... or just making yourself dizzy for fun.

Moulin de la Galette (Montmartre) – The Windmill that Witnessed a Massacre – Perched on Montmartre are two historic windmills, remnants of its farming past. The most famous, Moulin de la Galette, isn't just known from Renoir's paintings – it survived a gruesome chapter during the 1814 siege of Paris. The mill's owner, Monsieur Debray, defended his windmill against Cossack invaders. He and his sons were killed, and legend says the Cossacks nailed Debray's corpse to the blades of the windmill in revenge. (So much for windmills being peaceful!) Today the Moulin de la Galette is part of a restaurant, and the sails no longer turn. But you can view it at 83 Rue Lepic and imagine the battle that took place here. Montmartre's quirky charm often belies its blood-soaked history – even a postcard-perfect windmill has a dark tale to tell.

145 Rue La Fayette (10th Arr.) – The Fake Building That's Actually a Vent – At first glance, 145 Rue La Fayette looks like a normal Haussmannian apartment block – until you realize the windows are pitch-black and there are no balconies. In fact, it's a false façade hiding a huge air shaft for the RER B suburban train line below. The "building" is only a few feet deep; behind its walls rush train tunnels and ventilation equipment. Paris built several such fake facades to preserve the pretty uniform look of streets while accommodating modern infrastructure. This one has closed shutters painted on and dummy doors – a literal house of cards. If you linger, you might feel vibrations from the trains. It's a fun secret to impress friends: "See that house? It's not a house at all!" Talk about Parisian stagecraft – even the architecture wears a mask.

Deyrolle (Rue du Bac) – The Taxidermy Time Capsule – Part natural history museum, part curiosity shop, Deyrolle has been operating since 1831 and feels like stepping into a Wes Anderson film. Wander its creaky wooden floors amid hundreds of stuffed animals – from butterflies and beetles under glass to a full-size lion and polar bear. Salvador Dalí and Nabokov found inspiration here, and indeed it's an "educational" store where almost everything is for sale or rent (need a zebra for your party? They've got you). In 2008, a devastating fire charred much of the collection – leaving a haunting scene of singed feathers and sooty fur. But thanks to worldwide donations, Deyrolle rose from the ashes, restored to its 19th-century glory. Today it's open to the public – you can browse, take photos, even buy an ethically sourced taxidermy specimen. It's delightfully weird and utterly enchanting, a place where science meets art meets Victoriana. (Just remember, the tigers are not for petting!)

Square René Viviani (5th Arr.) – The Oldest Tree in Paris – In this little Left Bank park by Shakespeare & Co. bookstore stands a gnarled robinia pseudoacacia tree planted in 1601 by royal gardener Jean Robin. Over 420 years old, it's the grandpa of all Parisian trees. It has survived wars, revolutions, and pollution – though not without scars. Its trunk is split and largely hollow now, propped up by concrete and wooden crutches. But incredibly, it still blooms with cascades of white flowers every spring! Locals call it "le doyen des arbres" (dean of the trees). The tree witnessed medieval Paris transform into the city of today, and legend says it symbolizes resilience. A sign nearby notes its venerable age. Have a seat on a bench and pay respects to this living time traveler – a leafy link to the days of Shakespeare and Marie de Médicis.

Bar Hemingway (Ritz Hotel) – "Libération" 1944 and 51 Martinis – When Paris was liberated from the Nazis in August 1944, war correspondent Ernest Hemingway famously "liberated" the Ritz Hotel's bar in person. Hemingway arrived with Resistance fighters and demanded the bartender serve them martinis – lots of them. According to lore (and the Ritz's own tribute), he racked up a tab for 51 dry martinis in one epic sitting! In truth, he probably had help consuming those, but the exploit became legend. Today the Ritz's

Bar Hemingway – named in his honor – is a cozy, wood-paneled shrine to the writer, filled with memorabilia. Order a dry martini (maybe not 51 of them) and toast to Papa Hemingway. As the man himself said, "I drink to make other people more interesting." At Bar Hemingway, the stories practically pour themselves.

Palais de Chaillot Tunnels (Trocadéro) – The Secret 2004 Cinema – Parisian explorers pulled off a cinematic caper beneath the Trocadéro. In 2004, police on a training exercise stumbled upon a hidden underground cinema-cum-restaurant in a large cavern under Chaillot. They found a full-size movie screen, projection equipment, a stocked bar and tables – even electricity and phone lines running mysteriously into the earth. Caught off guard, the police returned days later with electrical experts, only to find everything gone and a note lying in the empty cave that read: "Do not try to find us." A clandestine art group called Les UX eventually claimed credit for the covert cinema. They'd been hosting secret film screenings in the catacombs. The incident caused a stir, proving that beneath Paris's streets, subversive creativity thrives literally underground. (To this day, the catacomb cinema's movies and attendees remain a ghostly mystery.)

Pont Neuf (Île de la Cité) – Henry IV's Time Capsule Statue – The bronze equestrian statue of King Henry IV at Pont Neuf has a story almost as rich as the Henry IV legends. The original 1614 statue was destroyed in the Revolution, and a new one was erected in 1818. During its installation, workers discovered a surprise hidden in the pedestal: a time capsule with letters and mementos from over two centuries earlier. These artifacts (placed by 18th-century restorers) were intended for "future generations" – a secret message from the past. When the statue was restored again in 2004, another capsule of documents from 1818 was reportedly found, including newspapers and a royal seal. Today, the bronze king gazes over Pont Neuf, and lovers mingle in Square du Vert-Galant below. Most have no idea a little treasure trove once hid inside the statue's base. Henry IV's monument literally contains history – a fitting tribute to a king who always had something up his sleeve.

Les Puces de Saint-Ouen (Clignancourt) – Origin of the "Flea Market" – Paris's sprawling antiques bazaar, the Marché aux Puces, literally means "market of the fleas" – and yup, it's because the second-hand clothes for sale there were reputedly infested with critters in the old days. In the late 19th century, rag-and-bone men gathered here outside the city walls to sell junk and used garments salvaged from Parisian trash. Shoppers joked about the flea-bitten merchandise, giving the market its colorful name. Despite (hopefully) far fewer fleas today, the name stuck and spread worldwide as "flea market." Saint-Ouen's Puces, established officially in 1885, is now the world's largest antiques market – a warren of stalls offering everything from vintage Paris posters to Napoleon's old mirror. The only bites you'll get are from the merchants if you haggle poorly. It's open weekends, and exploring its maze-like alleys is like a treasure hunt – you never know what odd object (or etymological history) you'll find.

La Petite Ceinture (Various Arrondissements) – The Abandoned Railway Belt – Snaking around Paris is an old 32 km rail line called La Petite Ceinture ("Little Belt"), which operated from 1852 to 1934 as a circular passenger railway. Once vital, it became obsolete and was largely abandoned, left to quietly rust and be reclaimed by nature. For decades it was a paradise for urban explorers: graffiti artists, secret picnickers, and foxes colonized the overgrown tracks. In recent years, portions have been sensitively reopened as public walking trails and parks – you can stroll the tracks in the 15th or 16th arrondissements, for example. It's surreal to walk on silent rails with trees and wildflowers, knowing trains once chugged here full of Victorian commuters. The Petite Ceinture is Paris's answer to New York's High Line, just with more wild charm. Keep an eye out for ghostly station platforms and vintage railway signs peeking through the greenery. It's a ribbon of secret greenery encircling the City of Light.

Rue du Chat-qui-Pêche (Latin Quarter) – Narrowest Street in Paris (and a Cat Legend) – This whimsically named lane ("Street of the Fishing Cat") holds the title of Paris's narrowest street – a mere 1.8 m wide at its skinniest. Essentially an alley sloping down to the Seine, it was built in 1540 and barely fits two people side by side. Its fanciful name comes from an old shop sign depicting a cat catching a fish. Local legend adds spice: a 15th-century alchemist named Dom Perlet lived here with a mysterious black cat that people often saw "fishing" in the river. Suspecting witchcraft, some students killed the cat... only to later encounter Dom Perlet alive and well – and his cat back from the dead! The superstitious folks believed the devil was involved and left the alchemist alone. Today Rue du Chat-qui-Pêche is an unremarkable cobbled passage (no witch's lair in sight), but it sparks the imagination. Walk through – three steps and you're done – and you can say you traversed Paris's shortest and narrowest street with one quirky step.

Notre-Dame's Rooster (Île de la Cité) – Relic-Filled Weathervane Survives Fire – Atop Notre- Dame's spire sat a copper rooster weathervane, a symbol believed to protect Paris. Inside this rooster were holy relics: a fragment of the Crown of Thorns and relics of

Saint Denis and Saint Geneviève. When Notre-Dame caught fire in April 2019, the flaming spire collapsed – and the rooster was presumed lost. Miraculously, amidst the charred debris the next day, workers found the rooster battered but intact. The precious relics inside, having taken a 300-foot fall, survived as well. This copper cock had done its job protecting the holy items – and became a hopeful symbol of the cathedral's resilience. The original rooster, dented and scarred, will be displayed in the Notre-Dame Museum, while a replica now perches on the reconstructed spire. Keep that in mind when you see the shiny new rooster watching over Paris – it's the literal phoenix of Notre-Dame, risen from the ashes with a cock-a-doodle-doo.

***Saint-Sulpice Church* – The Gnomon "Rose Line" of *The Da Vinci Code* –** Inside the grand Saint-Sulpice, a brass meridian line runs across the floor to a towering obelisk – an 18th-century astronomical instrument known as the Gnomon of Saint-Sulpice. It was built in the 1740s to determine the exact date of Easter each year by tracking sunbeams at the equinox. If this sounds familiar, it's because Dan Brown mis-labels it the "Rose Line" in *The Da Vinci Code*, sparking all kinds of fictional intrigue. In reality, it's not a mysterious pagan relic but a "wonderful piece of old-fashioned technology" for calendar-making. A small lens in a window projects a disk of sunlight along the line at noon. On the spring equinox, the sunspot hits a specific brass plate, and voilá – Easter's timing is confirmed. Fiction aside, you can visit Saint-Sulpice (free entry) and see the brass line and obelisk for yourself. Just remember: the only secret this "Rose Line" hides is a lesson in astronomy – no albino monks required.

***Mur des Fédérés (Père Lachaise)* –** The Communards' Last Stand – Deep in Père Lachaise cemetery stands a somber stone wall with a simple plaque – yet it's a crucible of French history. In May 1871, at the end of the Paris Commune uprising, 147 socialist revolutionaries (the Federates) made their final stand in these cemetery grounds. Defeated, they were lined up against a wall and executed en masse by the Versailles troops. This became known as the Mur des Fédérés. For generations, it's been a pilgrimage site for leftists – every year on May 28, people gather to lay red flowers and sing in memory of the Commune's martyrs. You can still see the pockmarks of bullets on the wall's stones. Standing there, you feel how a peaceful cemetery turned into a last battlefield. It's a powerful, under-the-radar spot that quietly tells of liberty, hope, and tragedy. (Also a good reminder that Père Lachaise isn't just famous rockstars – it holds the drama of France itself.)

Les Innocents (Les Halles) – The Stinking Cemetery and the Birth of the Catacombs – In the 1700s, the Cimetière des Innocents near Les Halles was so overstuffed with bodies that it literally oozed corruption – neighborhood cellars were foul from "adipocere" (corpse wax) seeping through soil. By 1780, a mass grave collapse spilled rotting corpses next door, and the public had had it. The solution? The city exhumed millions of bones and transferred them to former quarry tunnels – creating the Catacombs in 1786. Les Innocents cemetery was closed and converted into a market and park. Today you can find Fountain of the Innocents in a lively square where once a mountain of skulls stood. A sign marks the site's history. Without this "great stench" of Les Innocents, Paris might not have its famous Catacombs. Next time you're browsing shops at Les Halles, recall that beneath your feet was once a teeming, noxious city of the dead – cleared only when folks literally couldn't stand the smell of their ancestors.

Panthéon (Latin Quarter) – Foucault's Pendulum and Earth's Rotation – In 1851, physicist Léon Foucault hung a 67 m pendulum from the Panthéon's dome and gave Paris a scientific spectacle: as the pendulum swung, its plane of motion slowly rotated, proving the Earth spins on its axis. Crowds marveled as the pendulum's tip traced out the rotation – a simple but elegant demonstration of a concept that had been hard to visualize. Foucault's original pendulum bob now resides in a museum, but the Panthéon often displays a working replica of the pendulum under its dome. Visitors can watch the golden bob swing serenely and imagine the excitement of those 19th-century Parisians seeing science swing into action. The device was so iconic it featured in Umberto Eco's novel Foucault's Pendulum. Tip: if you visit when it's on display, note the pins or sand patterns it knocks over to show the rotation. It's a quietly thrilling bit of history and physics in one – where revolutionary heroes lie entombed, a different kind of revolution (Earth's) is perpetually on display above.

Moulin Rouge (Pigalle) – Le Pétomane: The Fartiste of Montmartre – The Belle Époque's famed cabaret, the Moulin Rouge, saw many extraordinary acts – but none as bizarre as Le Pétomane, the professional farter. Joseph Pujol was a mild-mannered baker with an unusual talent: he could inhale air (or water) and expel it from his rear with perfect control, emitting musical notes and sound effects on command. In 1892, dressed in a smart red coat and white gloves, he took to the Moulin Rouge stage and proceeded to "play" the crowd: little toots to warm up, a dainty "bride's fart" to make genteel ladies blush, even a 10-second colonic cannon blast that brought down the house. Women in corsets swooned with laughter, nurses carried some out as Pujol's act literally knocked 'em dead. Despite the indelicate subject, Le Pétomane's performances were reportedly odorless (he did an enema beforehand) and surprisingly sophisticated – a true art form. The fact that one of Montmartre's biggest stars was a fart artist speaks volumes about Parisian humor. Today, the Moulin Rouge's flashy can-can show continues – slightly less flatulent but every bit as committed to joyous absurdity.

Poste Pneumatique (underground network) – The Victorian "Internet" of Tubes – Long before emails, Paris had a pneumatic tube mail system that was essentially a 19th-century internet beneath the streets. Starting in 1866, the Poste Pneumatique used pressurized air tubes to shoot canisters containing telegrams and letters all across the city's 89 tubes. By the 1930s this network stretched over 400 km of tubes snaking through sewers and tunnels. Messages zipped from Montmartre to Montparnasse in minutes – no traffic jams under here. Amazingly, the pneumatic post remained in operation until 1984, when faxes and computers finally rendered it obsolete. At its height, millions of "pneumograms" were sent annually, and you could even mail a love letter via tube for same-hour delivery to your cherie across town. Today, remnants of the system (like tube terminals) can be seen in some old post offices and the Postal Museum. The idea of thousands of little capsules whizzing beneath Paris feels delightfully steampunk – a reminder that the City of Light once thrived on the whoosh of air pressure carrying on its whispers.

Canal Saint-Martin – The Great Canal Cleanup and Its Sunken Treasures – Every 10–15 years, Paris drains the 4.5 km Canal Saint-Martin for cleaning, and the spectacle of the muddy canal bed yields astonishing junk. When the canal was emptied in 2016, curious crowds gaped at mountains of trash and treasure pulled from the muck. Among the haul: 90 of those Vélib' rental bikes (bien sûr), dozens of regular bikes and scooters, traffic signs, park benches, hundreds of wine bottles (cheers!), shopping carts, ghostly boomboxes, even at least one loaded handgun and unexploded World War I shells. In a previous 2001 cleanup they found safes, gold coins, a bathtub, and an entire car. It seems Parisian canals double as bottomless lost-and-found bins. The city removed 45 tons of debris in 2016, then refilled the canal with fresh water and fish. Today the canal is again a picturesque spot where hipsters sip wine on the banks – just know beneath those gentle waters lies a modern archaeological trove of Parisian life (and perhaps a few stolen scooters awaiting the next dredging).

Pont des Arts – Love Locks and a Bridge Too Far (Weight) – In the 2000s, tourists began clipping padlocks to the mesh railings of the Pont des Arts footbridge, symbolizing eternal love (keys tossed into the Seine). Sweet at first, this trend exploded into an ecological and safety nightmare. By 2015, an estimated 700,000 "love locks" weighing 45 tons bowed the bridge dangerously. A section of railing even collapsed under the weight (no lovers were harmed). The city, saying "C'est assez!", hired crews to remove all the locks in June 2015 – it took several trips by crane to haul away the 45 tonnes of metal. The mesh panels were then replaced with glass to prevent re- locking. The salvaged cadenas d'amour were auctioned for charity – broken hearts supporting good causes. You can still visit the Pont des Arts for a romantic moment with gorgeous Seine views, but sorry lovebirds: your lock has lost the key to this bridge. Better stick to selfies and kisses – lighter on the infrastructure!

Place de la Concorde (formerly Place de la Révolution) – Guillotine Gossip and a Blushing Head – This grand square saw some ghastly scenes during 1793–94 when the Revolutionary guillotine stood here, sending nearly 2,800 people (including King

Louis XVI and Marie Antoinette) to their deaths. One infamous anecdote: when Charlotte Corday (who assassinated Marat) was beheaded, the executioner's assistant lifted her severed head from the basket and slapped her cheek. Spectators swore the head's face flushed red with indignation, an eerie "proof" that a moment of consciousness persisted after decapitation. (Scientists of the time debated if guillotined heads could still see or think for a few seconds – creepy!) This tale of the blushing, blinking head became legend. Today Place de la Concorde is all luxury hotels and an Egyptian obelisk, with barely a hint of the blood that once soaked its soil. But if you stand by the obelisk where the scaffold stood, you might imagine the roar of the crowd and that executioner's slap echoing through history – one of Paris's grisliest lore.

Bibliothèque Nationale (Richelieu site) – Marie Curie's Radioactive Notebooks – Among the Bibliothèque Nationale's most fascinating holdings are the personal papers of Marie Curie – two-time Nobel laureate and pioneering physicist. But you can't just thumb through her lab notebooks from the 1890s... because they are highly radioactive. Curie's research with radium and polonium contaminated her belongings so thoroughly that her notebooks, clothes, even her cookbook will remain dangerous for another 1,500 years. The papers are kept in lead-lined boxes in Paris's national library, and anyone who wants to consult them must sign a waiver and wear protective gear. It's surreal: these decades-old pages are essentially nuclear waste. In life, Curie used to carry test tubes of radium in her pockets, giving off a ghostly glow. The price of that brilliance is seen today in those notebook pages that still sizzle with ionizing radiation. They are both scientific treasures and enduring hazards – a poignant testament to Curie's luminous and lethal legacy.

Catacombs Concert of 1897 (Port-Mahon Gallery) – Macabre Midnight Serenade – One spring night in 1897, the Paris catacombs hosted perhaps the eeriest concert ever. About 100 adventurous souls descended by torchlight into the ossuary, where members of the Opera orchestra played a midnight concert among the skulls. The program? Fittingly morbid: Chopin's Funeral March and Saint-Saëns's Danse Macabre, echoing off the bone-lined walls. Invitees sat on stone ledges amidst femurs and skulls, listening to music about death literally surrounded by the dead. Newspapers reported the strange event, alternately thrilled and scandalized. Authorities were not amused – such use of the catacombs was unauthorized, and the organizers faced repercussions. Today, official catacombs tours end by 5 p.m., and throwing underground concerts is a big no-no. But the legend of that 1897 concert lingers as a true gothic tale. Next time you visit the catacombs, imagine strains of phantom violins and the clack of dancing skeletons – and be glad you surface with only a souvenir, not a serenade.

Harry's New York Bar (2nd Arr.) – Birthplace of the Bloody Mary – "Harry's Bar" in Paris is not just an expat watering hole – it's where one of the world's most famous cocktails was born. In 1921 bartender Fernand Petiot mixed up vodka and tomato juice with spices and dubbed it the Bloody Mary, reportedly in honor of a patron's girlfriend named Mary (or perhaps Queen Mary Tudor). Originally it was called "Bucket of Blood" (yikes), but thankfully "Bloody Mary" stuck. Ernest Hemingway and F. Scott Fitzgerald drank here; George Gershwin plinked out tunes on Harry's piano. The bar even claims to have invented other classics like the French 75 and Sidecar. Today Harry's, located at 5 Rue Daunou, looks much as it did a century ago – mahogany bar, American college pennants on the walls, and an easy mix of locals and travelers. Try a Bloody Mary at the source (it's delicious, not a bit bucket-of-blood-y) and toast to the little Paris bar that spiced up cocktail history. Hemingway once quipped, "If you want to know about a culture, spend a night in its bars." Harry's would be a fine choice.

Eiffel Tower – **The Man Who Sold It (Twice!)** – In 1925, con artist Victor Lustig pulled off a brazen scam: he "sold" the Eiffel Tower for scrap metal. Posing as a government official, Lustig convinced a scrap dealer that the city could no longer afford the Tower's upkeep and was secretly accepting bids to dismantle it. The dealer paid hefty bribes to secure this illicit contract – only to realize he'd been duped when Lustig vanished. Astoundingly, Lustig tried the same scam a month later with a different mark, nearly succeeding again ! Dubbed "the man who sold the Eiffel Tower twice," Lustig became a legend among grifters. Today the Tower stands strong (those rivets aren't going anywhere), but this episode is a favorite Parisian anecdote. Next time you're approached in Paris with a deal that's too good to be true – say, a gold ring "found" on the ground – think of Monsieur Lustig and politely decline. The Eiffel Tower is not for sale, mesdames et messieurs.

Luxor Obelisk (Place de la Concorde) – The "Broken" Gift Clock – The 3,300-year-old Luxor Obelisk at Concorde was a gift from Egypt in 1830. What did France give in return? A grand mechanical clock for the Cairo citadel – which, Egyptian lore has it, never worked properly. For over 175 years the clock (a large ornate tower) reportedly failed to keep accurate time, chiming out of sync or not at all. Egyptians joked that the French swindled them: trading a useless clock for a priceless obelisk. In reality, the clock did function sporadically (recently restored in 2021 after ages of disrepair). But the tale of the broken clock became part of Cairo folklore. Meanwhile, the pink granite obelisk – nicked from Luxor's temple of Ramses II – stands proudly in Paris, covered in hieroglyphs. Its twin stayed in Egypt. So if you think about it, Paris got one obelisk and Egypt got one lemon of a clock. C'est la vie! At least the obelisk doesn't tell time – it merely withstands it.

Top of the Eiffel Tower – **Gustave Eiffel's Secret Apartment** – High atop the Eiffel Tower, 285 meters above ground, in fact, Gustave Eiffel built himself a cozy little hideaway. The tower's designer included a private apartment on the third level, where he entertained VIP guests like Thomas Edison. The decor was modest: wooden furniture, paisley wallpaper, a piano – a stark contrast to the iron behemoth outside. Parisians of the day were jealous – many offered big money to rent the space, but Eiffel refused. He preferred to keep this lofty perch for scientific experiments and quiet reflection above the city's bustle. Today visitors can't go inside the apartment, but you can peek at it: there's a life-like wax tableau of Eiffel and Edison chatting over a phonograph. Look through the window on the top observation deck to spot this untouched 1889 time capsule. It's a delightful Easter egg of the tower: even in the world's most visited monument, Monsieur Eiffel carved out a little privacy with the best view in Paris.

Eiffel Tower (Champ de Mars) – Saved by Science and Radio – The Eiffel Tower was supposed to be a temporary showpiece for the 1889 World's Fair – planned to stand for 20 years and then be scrapped. By 1909, many Parisians indeed wanted the "ugly" iron giant torn down. How did it survive? Gustave Eiffel championed the tower's value for scientific experiments (like meteorology and astronomy) and, crucially, as a radio antenna. In 1903-1905, a permanent wireless telegraphy station was installed at the tower's summit. The tower's great height made it perfect for broadcasting signals. It soon became invaluable for the French military (intercepting crucial communications during World War I) and for early public radio. Its usefulness silenced the critics. The government simply couldn't pull down a strategic communication hub. Thus, Eiffel's 300 meter "temporary" structure became permanent. Next time you see it glittering at night, remember: if not for wireless technology, the Tower might have been melted into scrap by 1910. Instead, it's an enduring symbol of Paris – all thanks to a little bit of science and a lot of good signal.

"Is Paris Burning?" (Hotel Meurice, 1944) – The City that Escaped WWII Flames – As Allied forces neared Paris in August 1944, Hitler infamously ordered General Dietrich von Choltitz, the city's German military governor, to turn Paris into rubble rather than let it be liberated. Landmarks were wired with explosives; the Eiffel Tower, Louvre, and Notre-Dame were at risk. Legend (and history books) recount that Hitler telephoned von Choltitz on August 25, 1944, furiously demanding: "Brennt Paris?" ("Is Paris burning?"). The good news: von Choltitz, realizing the war was lost and unwilling to be the vandal of Paris, defied Hitler's orders and surrendered instead of destroying the city. Thus, Paris was liberated with its architectural treasures intact. The Hotel Meurice on Rue de Rivoli, where von Choltitz had his headquarters, was the scene of this high drama (today it's a five-star hotel; hard to imagine it as Nazi HQ). Because one general chose beauty over barbarism, the City of Light emerged from WWII virtually unscathed. Next time you stroll the Seine, be grateful – Paris was minutes from burning, but by a minor miracle it was saved.

Rue des Degrés (2nd Arr.) – The Shortest Street in Paris – Blink and you'll miss it: Rue des Degrés is only 5.75 m long and consists entirely of one short flight of stairs connecting Rue Beauregard to Rue Clery. This teeny "street" has no addresses (except maybe the door at the top). Its name literally means Street of Steps. There's no romantic legend or ghost story here – just the novelty of Paris's tiniest thoroughfare. It dates from the 17th century when it provided access up a slope in the old city walls. Now it's basically 14 stone steps with a handrail. Tourists seeking quirky photo-ops hunt it down for a quick snap – standing in the middle you can touch both side walls. Sure, it's not a grand site, but in a city of sweeping boulevards, there's something charming about a "street" you can traverse in two seconds flat. Find it in the 2nd arrondissement and tread where countless Parisians have – though given its size, probably not too many at once.

51 Rue de Montmorency (3rd Arr.) – Nicolas Flamel's House (Alchemy Legend) – Tucked in the Marais is a medieval house from 1407, claimed to be the oldest stone house in Paris – and it belonged to Nicolas Flamel, a famed alchemist. Yes, the same Flamel name-dropped in Harry Potter was a real person. He was a scribe and manuscript-seller, and after his death a legend grew that he had discovered the Philosopher's Stone and achieved immortality by turning lead into gold. (There's no proof he actually did this – he died in 1418 – but gossip of hidden alchemical texts swirled for centuries.) The house at No. 51 still stands, with its Gothic inscription intact: Flamel had carved on the facade that the house was built for the poor to lodge in for free. Today it's a restaurant (L'Auberge Nicolas Flamel), so you can literally dine in a sorcerer's supposed abode. The wooden beams and limestone walls inside are authentic. Try not to spill your wine – you never know if it might transmute into something special. And if the waiter seems very old... maybe Flamel really did crack that immortality thing after all.

Harry's Bar – The French 75 and Other Cocktail Legends – Another one from Harry's New York Bar, because this joint overflowed with mixological innovation. The French 75 cocktail (gin, champagne, lemon) was invented here around WWI, named after the French 75mm artillery gun due to its kick. The Sidecar (brandy, Cointreau, lemon) also has a Paris origin story – often attributed to the Ritz Bar around 1920, but Harry's likes to claim a version of it too. Even the Bloody Mary's etymology is debated: one story says Hemingway asked for a drink that wouldn't smell of alcohol so his wife Mary wouldn't nag – thus a neutral tomato juice base gave "Bloody Mary" her name. What's certain is that Harry's Bar – which opened in 1911 and has been serving ever since (even through Prohibition, by being in Paris!) – is a crucible of cocktail history. It's where Gershwin composed An American in Paris and where expats wrote novels over drinks. Walk in today and not much has changed: you can still sit on a red stool, order a classic cocktail born on the premises, and toast to the bygone legends who drank in the very same spot. Cheers to santé and a century of liquid courage in the City of Light!

Complete List of 50 Quirky Tales & Hidden Gems of Paris – Sorted by Arrondissement

Place	Address	Closest Metro	Arrondissement
Jardin des Tuileries -- The "Little Red Man" Ghost	Place de la Concorde, 75001 Paris	Tuileries, Concorde	1st
Point Zéro des Routes de France (Notre-Dame Parvis)	Parvis Notre-Dame, 75001 Paris	Cité	1st
Palais de Justice (includes Sainte-Chapelle)	8 Boulevard du Palais, 75001 Paris	Cité, Saint-Michel	1st
12 Rue Chabanais	12 Rue Chabanais, 75002 Paris	Quatre-Septembre, Opéra	2nd
Harry's New York Bar -- Birthplace of the Bloody Mary	5 Rue Daunou, 75002 Paris	Opéra	2nd
Rue des Degrés -- The Shortest Street in Paris	Rue des Degrés, 75002 Paris	Étienne Marcel	2nd

Bibliothèque Nationale (Richelieu site) -- Marie Curie's Radioactive Notebooks	58 Rue de Richelieu, 75002 Paris	Bourse, Quatre-Septembre	2nd
51 Rue de Montmorency -- Nicolas Flamel's House (Alchemy Legend)	51 Rue de Montmorency, 75003 Paris	Rambuteau, Arts et Métiers	3rd
Notre-Dame Cathedral -- The Devil's Doorway (Biscornet's Wrought Iron); Relic-Filled Weathervane Survives Fire	6 Parvis Notre-Dame, 75004 Paris	Cité, Saint-Michel	4th
Rue Chanoinesse (Île de la Cité) -- Sweeney Todd of Paris (Medieval Legend)	Rue Chanoinesse, 75004 Paris	Cité	4th
Square de l'Île-de-France (Ile de la Cité)	Square de l'Île-de-France, 75004 Paris	Cité, Pont Neuf	4th
Pont Neuf -- Henry IV's Time Capsule Statue	Pont Neuf, 75004 Paris	Pont Neuf	4th

Les Innocents (Les Halles) -- The Stinking Cemetery and the Birth of the Catacombs	Place Joachim-du-Bellay, 75001 Paris	Châtelet-Les Halles	4th
Arènes de Lutèce -- A Roman Arena in Paris	49 Rue Monge, 75005 Paris	Place Monge, Cardinal Lemoine	5th
René Viviani -- The Oldest Tree in Paris	Square René Viviani, 75005 Paris	Saint-Michel, Maubert-Mutualité	5th
Panthéon -- Foucault's Pendulum and Earth's Rotation	Place du Panthéon, 75005 Paris	Cardinal Lemoine, Luxembourg	5th
Rue du Chat-qui-Pêche -- Narrowest Street in Paris (and a Cat)	Rue du Chat-qui-Pêche, 75005 Paris	Saint-Michel	5th
Le Procope (Latin Quarter) -- Napoleon's Forgotten Hat	13 Rue de l'Ancienne Comédie, 75006 Paris	Odéon	6th
Saint-Sulpice Church -- The Gnomon "Rose Line"	Place Saint-Sulpice, 75006 Paris	Saint-Sulpice	6th

Deyrolle (Rue du Bac) -- The Taxidermy Time Capsule	46 Rue du Bac, 75007 Paris	Rue du Bac	7th
Eiffel Tower -- The Man Who Sold It (Twice!); Gustave Eiffel's Secret Apartment; Saved by Science and Radio	Champ de Mars, 5 Avenue Anatole France, 75007 Paris	Bir-Hakeim, Trocadéro	7th
Luxor Obelisk (Place de la Concorde) -- The "Broken" Gift Clock	Place de la Concorde, 75008 Paris	Concorde	7th
Place de la Concorde (formerly Place de la Révolution) -- Guillotine Gossip and a Blushing Head	Place de la Concorde, 75008 Paris	Concorde	8th
Flame of Liberty (Alma Bridge)	Place de l'Alma, 75008 Paris	Alma-Marceau	8th
Palais Garnier (Opéra House)	Place de l'Opéra, 75009 Paris	Opéra	9th

145 Rue La Fayette	145 Rue La Fayette, 75010 Paris	Gare du Nord	10th
Canal Saint-Martin -- The Great Canal Cleanup and Its Sunken Treasures	Canal Saint-Martin, 75010 Paris	République	10th
Paris Catacombs (Denfert-Rochereau) -- Lost Man and Haunted	1 Avenue du Colonel Henri Rol-Tanguy, 75014 Paris	Denfert-Rochereau	14th
Catacombs Concert of 1897 (Port-Mahon Gallery) -- Macabre Midnight Serenade	1 Avenue du Colonel Henri Rol-Tanguy, 75014 Paris	Denfert-Rochereau	14th
Palais de Chaillot Tunnels (Trocadéro) -- The Secret 2004 Cinema	1 Place du Trocadéro, 75016 Paris	Trocadéro	16th
Place Marcel-Aymé (Montmartre)	Place Marcel-Aymé, 75018 Paris	Abbesses, Lamarck-Caulaincourt	18th

Place Dalida (Montmartre) -- The Shiny-Bosomed Bust	Place Dalida, 75018 Paris	Lamarck-Caulaincourt	18th
Clos Montmartre (Montmartre)	Rue des Saules, 75018 Paris	Rue des Saules, 75018 Paris	18th
Moulin de la Galette (Montmartre)	83 Rue Lepic, 75018 Paris	Abbesses, Lamarck-Caulaincourt	18th
Moulin Rouge (Pigalle) -- Le Pétomane: The Fartiste of Montmartre	82 Boulevard de Clichy, 75018 Paris	Blanche, Pigalle	18th
Théâtre du Grand-Guignol (Pigalle) (Note: Theatre no longer exists, but was in this area)	20 bis Rue Chaptal, 75009 Paris	Pigalle, Saint-Georges	18th
Père Lachaise Cemetery -- The Fertility Grave of Victor Noir	16 Rue du Repos, 75020 Paris	Père Lachaise, Philippe Auguste	20th
Mur des Fédérés (Père Lachaise) -- The Communards' Last Stand	16 Rue du Repos, 75020 Paris	Père Lachaise, Philippe Auguste	20th

Les Puces de Saint-Ouen (Clignancourt) -- Origin of the "Flea Market"	Rue des Rosiers, 93400 Saint-Ouen	Porte de Clignancourt	Suburbs
Musée des Vampires (Les Lilas)	14 Rue Jules David, 93260 Les Lilas	Mairie des Lilas	Suburbs
Arago Medallions (All Over Paris)	Various locations across all arrondissements	Various stations	All Over Paris
La Petite Ceinture (Various Arrondissements) -- The Abandoned Railway Belt	Various access points across multiple arrondissements	Various stations	All Over Paris
Poste Pneumatique (underground network) -- The Victorian "Internet" of Tubes	Underground network throughout central Paris	Various stations	All Over Paris
Paris Sewers (Égouts Museum)	Pont de l'Alma, 75007 Paris	Alma-Marceau	All Over Paris

Pont des Arts -- Love Locks and a Bridge Too Far (Weight)	Pont des Arts, 75001/75006 Paris	Louvre – Rivoli, Pont Neuf	All Over Paris

Part III:
House Secrets &
Château Escapes

Because nothing tells the true story of a city quite like its homes. This section is for design lovers, architecture nerds, and curious souls. Peek at the facades of legendary Parisian residences, visit homes that belonged to famous creatives, and escape the city on day trips to jaw-dropping châteaux, each with its own story, secrets, and splendor.

Whether you're planning your first trip or your fifteenth, whether you prefer strolling aimlessly or mapping out every moment—I hope you'll find inspiration in these pages. This is Paris for the curious, the romantic, the beauty-seekers and story-lovers.

So grab your metro pass, your most comfortable shoes (but make them cute), and let's wander with intention—and a little mischief.

If These Walls Could Whisper...

Paris wears its history like a well-cut coat—timeless, tailored, and always ready to surprise you with what's hidden in the lining. And while the Eiffel Tower and the Louvre get all the spotlight, the real stories of Paris—its heartbreaks and revolutions, salons and scandals—are tucked inside its homes.

This section is your invitation to slip through the keyholes.

Why Houses?

Because houses tell the truth, they are where history gets personal, where revolutions were whispered over dinner, where poems were scribbled by candlelight, where secret lovers slipped in through the back garden gate. Parisian houses—grand hôtels particuliers, artist garrets, even crumbling façades with stories to spare—reveal the soul of the city better than any monument can.

What Makes a Home Worth Visiting?

In a word: stories. And Paris is overflowing with them. From bold interiors designed by trailblazing architects to discreet apartments once home to literary legends or political mischief-makers, each address in this guide earned its place. Some are celebrated for their lush gardens or art collections. Others are famous for a single dramatic moment. And a few? Well, they simply have that ineffable Parisian je ne sais quoi.

Expect to discover:

- The palace with a secret tunnel built for Napoleon III's affairs.

- The sun-drenched atelier where Monet painted...and gossiped.

- The hauntingly beautiful home where a queen's ghost is said to wander.

- Châteaux that are less Versailles, more vibes and vineyards.

How to Use This Section

This isn't a checklist; it's an adventure. Some houses are open for full tours, with velvet ropes and museum gift shops. Others are private homes you'll admire from the sidewalk while sipping a café crème nearby. Many are tucked into neighborhoods perfect for an afternoon stroll. And some sit just beyond the city limits—easy day trips that deliver history and charm without the tourist chaos.

Use this book like a curious flâneur with excellent taste:

- Plot your visit around an open house or château tour.

- Take a self-guided walk and peek at façades that witnessed revolutions, love affairs, and artistic awakenings.

- Or sit in a garden café next door and imagine what the walls might say if only they could speak.

Because in Paris, they almost do.

* All addresses are documented and organized (by arrondissement, including metro stops) at the end of this section.

Beyond the Boulevards: Château Day Trips That Dazzle

Design, drama, and countryside escapes—just a train ride from the City of Light.

Château de Chantilly

Location: Chantilly – 50 minutes from Paris by train (Gare du Nord)

Open to the public (closed Tuesdays)

If Versailles is the overachieving older sibling of Parisian day trips, Château de Chantilly is the underrated middle child with great taste, an art collection that rivals the Louvre, and a pastry legacy. Yes, this is the birthplace of Chantilly cream—light as a cloud and far superior to anything you've ever squirted from a can.

Designed in the Renaissance style with classical updates, the château rises dreamily from a moat-like pond, complete with a drawbridge, swan-frequented waters, and endless French garden drama (designed by André Le Nôtre, who also did Versailles—he was *booked and busy* in the 17th century). Inside, the decor is peak aristocratic maximalism: think frescoed ceilings, gold trim, plush velvet, and one of the finest private libraries in France.

But here's the kicker: the art gallery (Musée Condé) holds over 800 Old Masters, including works by Raphael, Delacroix, and Ingres—all hung salon-style, floor-to-ceiling, in rooms so rich you might temporarily forget you ever liked minimalism. And it's all thanks to Henri d'Orléans, Duke of Aumale, who bequeathed it with the condition that nothing ever be moved. (Control freaks everywhere, take note.)

Fun fact: If you book the on-site restaurant, La Capitainerie, you can enjoy a proper French lunch with dessert made tableside—yes, with real Chantilly cream.

Design tip: Don't miss the Great Stables, where the aristocracy once pampered their horses more than most of us pamper ourselves. It now houses a *living horse museum* and offers equestrian performances under chandeliers. Because, of course.

Villa Savoye

Location: Poissy – 1 hour from Paris by train (Line J from Gare Saint-Lazare + 15-min walk)

Open to the public (closed Mondays)

Welcome to a house that looks like it crash-landed from 1960s outer space but was, in fact, built in 1931. Designed by Le Corbusier, the high priest of modernist architecture, Villa Savoye is a bucket-list destination for design nerds and anyone who wants to say things like "pilotis" and "ribbon windows" in conversation.

This all-white modernist masterpiece sits on stilts in the middle of a grassy clearing like an alien queen in repose. The interior is a marvel of early 20th-century innovation: an open floor plan, color-blocked rooms, and a rooftop garden long before it was cool. It was built as a weekend home for the Savoye family... who, hilariously, didn't enjoy living in it because modernism forgot to include insulation. Fashion over function, baby.

Fun fact: The bathroom features a blue-tiled sunken tub placed right under a horizontal window—peak avant-garde indulgence, and arguably the first Instagram bathroom ever created.

Design tip: Walk the famous "architectural promenade" Le Corbusier intended—starting at the entry ramp and circling up to the roof terrace. It's part guided tour, part sacred design pilgrimage.

Château de Malmaison

Location: Rueil-Malmaison – 30 minutes by train from Gare Saint-Lazare + short bus/Uber

Open to the public (closed Tuesdays)

If you ever wondered how chic an Empress really lived, look no further than Château de Malmaison, the former residence of Joséphine Bonaparte—fashion icon, botanical queen, and the woman who said, "Sure, let's plant 200 rare roses and put a harp in every room."

Though modest in scale compared to Versailles, Malmaison drips in neoclassical charm. The interiors, restored with obsessive historical accuracy, include red velvet drawing rooms, Egyptian-inspired motifs (thanks to Napoleon's campaign), and Joséphine's own canopied bedchamber in romantic hues. The music room has been described as "a Regency dream," and the library? Piled high with leather-bound political intrigue.

Fun fact: Joséphine introduced hundreds of exotic plants and animals to France here—her gardens included black swans, kangaroos, and one confused ostrich. Take that, Versailles menagerie.

Design tip: Don't skip the gardens, especially in spring. Many of the original rose varieties have been re-cultivated, and the greenhouses are full of Joséphine's prized blooms. Bring tissues.

Château de Fontainebleau

Location: Fontainebleau (1 hour from Paris by train from Gare de Lyon)

Open to the public (closed Tuesdays)

While Versailles gets all the press, Fontainebleau is the grand old dame of French châteaux—opulent, enormous, and dripping in layers of power, scandal, and imperial flair. This palace has seen it all: kings, queens, emperors, abdications, and enough interior makeovers to rival an HGTV marathon.

Originally a 12th-century hunting lodge, Fontainebleau was transformed by a succession of French monarchs into an architectural mixtape of Renaissance, Baroque, and Neoclassical styles. The ballroom alone has a coffered ceiling, 16th-century frescoes, and a fireplace so massive you could roast an entire boar in it. Which they probably did.

Napoleon loved the place so much he called it "the true home of kings" and even signed his abdication here. His throne room still exists—glorious, gold, and gloriously over the top. Meanwhile, Marie Antoinette left her soft touch in the boudoirs, and Louis XV added entire wings when the old ones just weren't doing it anymore.

Fun fact: The horseshoe staircase outside the entrance is where Napoleon gave his famous farewell speech to his guards in 1814. You can stand on the very stones where that tearful drama unfolded—and then turn around and take a selfie with the most regal façade in the region.

Design tip: If you love wallpaper, woodwork, and massive chandeliers, this place will ruin you for modern interiors forever. Give yourself time—Fontainebleau is big. Like, wear-comfortable-shoes big.

Château de Vaux-le-Vicomte

Location: Maincy (1 hr 15 min by train from Gare de Lyon + taxi/Uber)

Open to the public; special candlelit evenings in summer

The cautionary tale of Vaux-le-Vicomte is practically a Netflix drama waiting to happen. In 1661, finance minister Nicolas Fouquet threw the party of the century for Louis XIV here—complete with a lavish dinner, fireworks, and Molière performing live. The next thing he knew? He was in prison for the rest of his life. The Sun King took one look at this dazzling château and said, "I'll take it from here."

And no wonder. Vaux-le-Vicomte is the château that inspired Versailles. Its architecture (by Louis Le Vau), gardens (André Le Nôtre), and interior decoration (Charles Le Brun) were so flawless together, they made Louis XIV jealous enough to ruin a man's life.

Today, the estate is privately owned but open to the public—and it is everything you want in a French château: domed pavilions, endless gardens, mirrored salons, and a library that looks straight out of *Beauty and the Beast*.

Fun fact: On summer Saturdays, the entire château and garden are illuminated by thousands of candles for a candlelight visit complete with classical music. It's like stepping into a baroque fever dream, minus the powdered wigs.

Design tip: Bring binoculars or a good zoom lens—Vaux's gardens are so perfectly symmetrical and vast that you'll want to see the full effect from above. Climb the dome for a panoramic view worthy of an 18th-century drone.

Château de Rambouillet

Location: Rambouillet (45 min from Paris by train from Gare Montparnasse)

Open to the public (closed Mondays)

Tucked into a forest and less famous than its glittery cousins, Rambouillet has been the site of royal hunts, presidential retreats, and an entire dairy palace built to impress Marie Antoinette. Yes, she had her own dairy built here—complete with marble churns—because rich girl hobbies have always been a thing.

Originally a medieval fortress, Rambouillet was redesigned over the centuries into a grand yet intimate residence. Louis XVI came for the hunting, Napoléon stopped by for the silence, and Charles de Gaulle reportedly disliked the wallpaper. But the best part? It still serves as the official presidential country estate—Macron has literally napped here.

Highlights include the Queen's Dairy (delightfully ridiculous), the Shell Cottage (a garden folly encrusted with real seashells), and a 200-acre forest that's open to strolling, lounging, or playing out your best aristocrat-in-hiding fantasy.

Fun fact: In 1975, Rambouillet hosted the very first G6 summit. Imagine all those heads of state nodding thoughtfully in rooms filled with gilded boiserie and tapestries of goats.

Design tip: The mix of rustic and refined is genuinely charming here. Think of it as Versailles' cooler, quieter cousin who vacations in the woods and always looks good in linen.

Château de Maisons (a.k.a. Maisons-Laffitte)

Location: Maisons-Laffitte (30 minutes from Paris by RER A or train from Gare Saint-Lazare)

Open to the public (closed Mondays)

If you've ever wondered what would happen if you gave a starchitect of the 17th century total creative freedom, behold Château de Maisons. Designed by François Mansart (yes, that Mansart—the guy who gave us the mansard roof), this château is basically the Beyoncé of French classicism: poised, powerful, and built to impress.

Completed around 1651 for René de Longueil, a man who clearly believed in flexing his wealth via limestone symmetry, the château became the blueprint for aristocratic homes for the next century. Louis XIV studied it. Versailles copied it. Interior decorators still reference it.

Inside, you'll find a grand staircase that feels like a cathedral and rooms packed with period detailing: gilded molding, intricate parquet floors, and trompe-l'œil ceilings that would give Michelangelo a run for his money. Every corner seems designed for dramatic cape-swishing entrances.

Fun fact: It briefly became a racehorse training center in the 19th century—because apparently, every château goes through a weird phase in its later years. Today, it's lovingly restored and blissfully quiet, even on weekends.

Design tip: Don't miss the Cabinet aux Miroirs (Mirror Room), where angled mirrors reflect a frescoed ceiling, so you don't crick your neck trying to admire it. Renaissance meets smart interior layout.

Château de Sceaux

Location: Sceaux (30–40 minutes by RER B from central Paris)

Open to the public; park open daily, château closed Mondays

Want Versailles vibes without the crowds and fainting tourists? Head to Château de Sceaux, where you'll find manicured French gardens, fountains, sculpture-lined pathways, and a château that feels less like a museum and more like a really luxurious invitation to slow down.

Originally built in the 17th century, the current château is a 19th-century reconstruction by the Duke of Trévise—but don't let that stop you. Inside is the Musée du Domaine Départemental de Sceaux, featuring classical paintings and lush interiors that strike a balance between formality and warmth.

The real showstopper, though, is outside. André Le Nôtre—France's favorite landscape artist—designed the gardens, which are textbook formal French but with just enough whimsy to keep things romantic. Tree-lined canals reflect the sky, terraced lawns invite picnics, and the spring cherry blossoms? Instagram heaven.

Fun fact: Sceaux hosts a cherry blossom festival every spring that turns the park into a sea of pink. Locals come dressed for full photo ops, and the vibe is pure joy with a side of rosé.

Design tip: The Orangery hosts exhibitions, and the garden's symmetry is a masterclass in geometric elegance. It's a dream location for design sketching, landscape inspiration, or your next author photo.

Château de Vincennes

Location: Vincennes (20 minutes from central Paris via Metro Line 1)

Open to the public daily

If you think medieval castles are reserved for far-flung fairy tales, think again. Château de Vincennes is right at the edge of Paris, and it is pure fortress fantasy—complete with a drawbridge, a deep moat, turrets, and a donjon (that's a fortified tower, not a Fifty Shades situation).

Dating back to the 14th century, this castle was once the royal residence before the Louvre got fancy. Charles V expanded it into a proper palace with high defensive walls and a chapel that later inspired Sainte-Chapelle in Paris. You can still visit the soaring donjon—the tallest medieval keep in Europe—and climb the stairs for a panorama that mixes Paris skyline with a hit of medieval brooding.

The interior rooms are mostly sparse now, but the proportions, stone detailing, and ghost-of-monarchs-past vibes are worth the visit. The Gothic royal chapel next door is dazzling and surprisingly intimate.

Fun fact: Louis XIV was born here, and several kings used it as a royal prison—Voltaire, the Marquis de Sade, and Diderot all did a stint. It's like a who's who of Enlightenment jailbirds.

Design tip: Visit in the late afternoon for dramatic shadows and fewer crowds. If you're sketching or photographing, the towers and geometric lines of the ramparts make for striking compositions.

Château de Compiègne

Location: Compiègne (1 hr 15 min from Paris by train from Gare du Nord)

Open to the public (closed Tuesdays)

If you're into places that look like they were designed for diplomatic power moves (because they were), then Château de Compiègne is your kind of day trip. Originally built for Louis XV and later remodeled for Napoleon I, this Neoclassical masterpiece sits at the edge of a sprawling forest and feels like a stately, gilded exhale.

Unlike some châteaux that pile on the heavy drapery and drama, Compiègne is restrained and elegant, kind of like Versailles' cooler, more composed cousin. The grand salons are decked in refined color palettes, glimmering chandeliers, and just enough marble to impress but not overwhelm. The private apartments of Napoleon and Empress Marie-Louise are richly preserved, with textiles that somehow haven't faded from their imperial glory.

Fun fact: The château houses not one but three museums—covering the palace, the Second Empire, and... carriages. Yes, there is an entire museum of historical carriages, including sleighs, coronation coaches, and royal vehicles you didn't know you needed to ogle.

Design tip: The furniture here is some of the finest Empire style in France—sleek lines, rich wood, and gilded details with sphinxes and laurel wreaths for days. Definitely bring a sketchbook or a fully charged phone if you're the mood board type.

Château de Monte-Cristo

Location: Le Port-Marly (1 hour from Paris by train from Gare Saint-Lazare + short walk or taxi)

Open to the public (seasonal; usually closed in winter, open Wed–Sun)

If you're craving a château with pure novelist flair, look no further than Château de Monte-Cristo, the totally extra home of Alexandre Dumas, author of The Count of Monte Cristo and The Three Musketeers. In fact, the whole place feels like a writer's fever dream come to life, with ivy-covered towers, literary puns carved into walls, and a private Gothic writing pavilion.

Built in 1846, the main house is a whimsical neo-Renaissance structure, complete with decorative turrets and cherub-laden façades. Inside, the decor is just as theatrical—painted ceilings, ornate woodwork, and portraits of Dumas himself looking dramatically wind-swept. The pièce de résistance? The Château d'If, a miniature Gothic castle set in the garden where Dumas wrote in solitude, presumably surrounded by wine, books, and self-importance.

Fun fact: Dumas threw wild parties here and once had to sell the place because he ran out of money—turns out being a bestselling author in the 1800s didn't come with a reliable royalty stream. Relatable.

Design tip: The gardens are surprisingly lush, with hidden paths and trickling fountains. Pack a picnic and a notebook—this place practically dares you to write your own novel.

Château de Breteuil

Location: Choisel (about 1 hour by car or 90 minutes by train + bus from Paris)

Open to the public (daily; guided tours recommended)

If you love storytelling and fancy interiors in equal measure, Château de Breteuil offers a perfect mashup: a gorgeous historic château filled with wax figures re-enacting scenes from both French history and fairy tales. Yes, you read that correctly—there's a full wing of this château dedicated to Puss in Boots and Sleeping Beauty, with elaborate tableaux and plenty of 18th-century décor to marvel at between scenes.

The Breteuil family has lived here for generations, and their ancestors were right in the thick of French and European politics. The rooms are richly furnished—embroidered silk wall coverings, period portraits, porcelain galore—but the real fun is how the château brings history to life (literally) with lifelike mannequins. There's even a scene with Marie Antoinette on a divan and Louis XVI looking just slightly confused.

Fun fact: During WWII, the family hid Jewish children here from the Nazis. Today, there's a memorial in the gardens—just one of many emotional and important touches that give this storybook place real heart.

Design tip: The gardens are divided into several themed areas, including a boxwood maze and views over the Vallée de Chevreuse. This is an ideal château for families, romantics, and fans of high-concept interiors with a side of whimsy.

Château de Courances

Location: Courances (1 hr. 15 min by car; not easily accessible by public transport)

Open to the public (weekends from April to November; guided house tours only)

Château de Courances is a quiet stunner. You may not hear it name-dropped like Versailles or Fontainebleau, but insiders know: this is one of the most photogenic, romantic estates in all of Île-de-France. A private residence still occupied by the aristocratic de Ganay family, Courances is known for its flawless symmetry, endless reflecting pools, and gardens that are, quite literally, dripping in history.

Built in the early 17th century, the château is a perfect example of Louis XIII-style architecture—classic red brick with limestone trim and rows of arched windows that seem designed for epic slow-motion entrances. But the true star is the garden, often called the most beautiful Renaissance water garden in France. There are 14 reflecting pools, all connected by underground hydraulic systems designed centuries ago. It's like Versailles on a mindfulness retreat.

Inside the house (guided tours only), you'll find lived-in elegance: tapestries, painted panels, and the kind of carefully aged furniture that interior designers would give up caffeine for. Despite its grandeur, there's a warmth to the rooms that makes you feel like you could actually curl up on the velvet settee and read a novel.

Fun fact: Coco Chanel was a frequent guest here, and Courances has been the site of multiple fashion shoots—including spreads in

Vogue and L'Officiel. Don't be surprised if you stumble upon a bridal shoot while you're there.

Design tip: Come for the scenery, stay for the Japanese garden hidden behind a moss-covered wall. Designed in the early 20th century, it adds an unexpected Zen layer to the otherwise perfectly French formality. It's like discovering a new room in a house you thought you knew.

Château de Dampierre-en-Yvelines

Location: Dampierre-en-Yvelines (about 1 hour by car from Paris; limited train access + taxi)

Open to the public; park and gardens open year-round, interior access varies

Château de Dampierre is Versailles' dreamy, slightly rebellious cousin—the one who quit politics to study landscape design and live in a palatial country house. Designed by Jules Hardouin-Mansart (the same architect behind much of Versailles), Dampierre was built for the Duc de Chevreuse in the 17th century and has maintained its restrained elegance ever since.

The house sits in the middle of a wide formal garden framed by canals and woods, with a curved horseshoe staircase that leads visitors up to a tall slate-roofed façade. Recently renovated, the interiors are slowly reopening to the public and are absolutely worth the wait: warm tones, intimate salons, and libraries that feel more lived-in than ceremonial.

What sets Dampierre apart is its extensive parkland, which spans miles and features forests, canals, and 18th-century follies. You can stroll, bike, or take a horse-drawn carriage through landscapes that feel cinematic in the best way.

Fun fact: This château was briefly owned by the Wendel family (as in steel magnates), and they left behind a layer of 20th-century luxury, including a hidden Art Deco billiard room that's the stuff of gentleman's club dreams.

Design tip: Check their schedule—special open days sometimes feature candlelit visits and talks from restoration experts. It's a chance to see the château evolving in real-time, and to explore rooms few people have ever seen.

Château de Saint-Jean-de-Beauregard

Location: Saint-Jean-de-Beauregard (45 minutes by car; not accessible by train)

Open to the public on select weekends, especially for garden events and heritage days.

A small but spectacular jewel of a château, Saint-Jean-de-Beauregard is best known for its exquisite walled kitchen garden—a rare example of a 17th-century potager still cultivated to historic perfection. Think heirloom tomatoes, espaliered pear trees, lavender hedges, and flower borders so vibrant they deserve their own Instagram account.

The château itself is modest by royal standards—more manor house than palace—but it's lovingly maintained, and the interiors are rich with painted beams, antique tapestries, and big sunny windows that overlook the formal courtyard and gardens. It feels like the country retreat you'd design if you were a poet with a trust fund and a love of jam-making.

Saint-Jean hosts several renowned events throughout the year, including plant festivals that attract top European horticulturists and garden designers. It's where chic Parisians in wide-brim hats go to buy tulip bulbs and rare iris seeds.

Fun fact: The original 17th-century dovecote (yes, a fancy house just for pigeons) is still standing and is one of the largest in France. Inside are hundreds of pigeon "apartments," like the Airbnb of the aristocratic bird world.

Design tip: Go during one of the spring or fall garden days, and you'll also get to explore pop-up boutiques in the château's stables and orangerie. It's part historic house tour, part French country lifestyle fantasy.

House Secrets: Parisian Homes with a Story to Tell

Famous façades, storied salons, and sidewalk secrets worth the detour.

1st Arrondissement – Louvre & Place Vendôme

Coco Chanel's Apartment – 31 Rue Cambon (Exterior only): Above Chanel's flagship boutique sits the chic apartment where fashion icon Coco Chanel entertained in the 1920s style. She had a mirrored Art Deco staircase leading up to this elegant second-floor flat, though amusingly, she preferred to actually sleep across the street at the Ritz (today you can rent the lavish "Coco Chanel Suite" there). The apartment itself was more salon than home, filled with lacquered screens, gilded lions, and camellia motifs reflecting her personal design touches. Not open to the public, it remains a private sanctum (the ground-floor Chanel boutique can be visited, but Chanel's private quarters can only be imagined from the street).

Frédéric Chopin's Last Residence – 12 Place Vendôme (Exterior only): In 1849, composer Frédéric Chopin spent his final days in a refined apartment here on Place Vendôme. A discreet plaque on the ornate façade (now a jeweler's shop) marks where he died on October 17, 1849. At the time, this was an upscale quartier; Chopin's candlelit salon hosted a few close friends as he, tragically ill, dictated wishes like having Mozart's Requiem at his funeral. Today, you can stand in the elegant square, designed by Louis XIV, and picture the frail genius "dying beyond his means" in this grand hôtel particulier. Only viewable from outside, the building's classical stone arches belie the poignant history within.

Colette's Palais-Royal Apartment – 9 Rue de Beaujolais (Exterior only): Tucked under the arcades of the Palais-Royal gardens is the apartment where the novelist Colette spent her final years. She first moved into a tiny entresol "lair" here in the 1920s and later acquired the larger first-floor flat abovea. From her south-facing windows, Colette delighted in watching the fountains and children playing in the Palais-Royal below. This elegant 18th-century building became her sanctuary – she wrote in bed each morning with the sounds of Paris drifting in. Private today, it's marked by a plaque. Pause in the tranquil Palais-Royal garden and imagine Colette at her window, listening to the laughter of schoolchildren and dreaming up her stories.

3rd Arrondissement – Le Marais

Nicolas Flamel's House – 51 Rue de Montmorency (Exterior / Restaurant): The oldest stone house in Paris, built in 1407 by the medieval writer and alchemist Nicolas Flamel, still stands on this narrow Marais street. Its carved inscription in Old French is visible on the façade, beseeching passers-by to pray for the souls of the poor who sheltered here. (Flamel, despite later legend, did not concoct a Philosopher's Stone here – he built this house as a charity lodging for destitute laborers.) Today, the ground floor hosts a restaurant (the Auberge Nicolas Flamel), letting visitors dine amid history. Interiors are not a museum, but you can admire the Gothic stone doorway, the eroded carved angels, and the famous inscription on the street side. It's a tangible slice of 15th-century Paris, steeped in mystery and myth.

Hôtel Carnavalet (Musée de l'Histoire de Paris) – 23 Rue de Sévigné (Open to the public): This grand Renaissance mansion, begun in 1548, later became home to letter-writer Madame de Sévigné (she lived here 1677–1696). Its ornate stone portals and courtyards survive from the 16th–17th centuries, with additions by architect Mansart, making it one of the Marais' oldest mansions. Today it's the Museum of Paris History (Carnavalet), freshly renovated in 2021, and entry is free. Strolling its period rooms, you'll find revolutionary relics, Art Nouveau shop signs, and even Marcel Proust's cork-lined bedroom. Don't miss Madame de Sévigné's salon, where her wit once sparkled amidst gilded boiseries. Open to visitors, Carnavalet offers both historical artifacts and the atmosphere of a private hôtel particulier – complete with formal French gardens in the rear.

Musée Picasso (Hôtel Salé) – 5 Rue de Thorigny (Open to the public): Behind the grand wrought-iron gate is the Hôtel Salé, a baroque 17th-century mansion known as "the Salty" because it was built in the 1650s by a wealthy salt-tax collector. With its ornate stone staircase and high-ceilinged salons, this building is itself a work of art – Bruno Foucart called it "the grandest, most extravagant" Parisian mansion of its era. Now it houses the Musée Picasso, holding over 5,000 works by Pablo Picasso. As you wander through opulent rooms (once rarely inhabited by its owners and often leased out), you'll encounter Picasso's paintings, sculptures, even scribbled love notes. Open to visitors, the museum juxtaposes Picasso's radical art against gilded 17th-century interiors – an extraordinary dialogue of old and modern. Keep an eye out for the sweeping "Escalier d'Honneur" (ceremonial staircase) and the lavish carved doorways as you contemplate Picasso's genius in this sumptuous setting.

Hôtel de Soubise (Archives Nationales) – 60 Rue des Francs-Bourgeois (Occasionally open for tours): The Prince de Soubise's 18th-century city palace boasts what many call the most breathtaking Rococo interiors in Paris. In the 1730s, architect Germain Boffrand created oval salons here for the prince and princess, including the glittering Salon de la Princesse, featuring gilded boiseries, mirrored panels, and ceiling canvases by Boucher. These rooms remain almost unchanged since 1740, serving as a time capsule of Louis XV-era luxury. The mansion's exterior is Baroque grandeur (originally built in 1704 on a medieval manor's site), and the cour d'honneur and formal garden are freely accessible. Today it houses part of the National Archives, so you can visit its museum and peek into some historic rooms decorated with cherubs and garlands. Public access is limited (except during heritage days or special exhibits), but even a glimpse of the Cour d'Honneur and the monumental, curved façade offers a taste of aristocratic Paris.

4th Arrondissement – Marais & Île Saint-Louis

Maison de Victor Hugo – 6 Place des Vosges (Open as museum): Overlooking the arcaded Place des Vosges, the famed novelist Victor Hugo lived on the 2nd floor of this mansion from 1832 to 1848. Today, his apartment is preserved as the Victor Hugo Museum, and stepping inside feels like visiting the set of Les Misérables. You can wander through Hugo's red-carpeted bedroom (complete with his writing desk and high canopy bed) and salons adorned with Chinese screens and Gothic Revival furniture of his own design. It's a personal, even quirky collection of décor reflecting Hugo's romantic imagination. Open to the public (free entry), the museum invites you to "enter the intimacy of his souvenirs, interior decoration and furniture". Stand by the window where Hugo once gazed out at the Vosges gardens, and you're literally in the author's footsteps – a must for literature lovers.

Hôtel de Sully – 62 Rue Saint-Antoine (Courtyard & Gardens open; interiors closed): This 1620s mansion is a peaceful oasis linking busy Rue Saint-Antoine to Place des Vosges. Built in Louis XIII style with warm stone, slate roofs, and sculpted allegories of the four seasons on its facades, it was purchased in 1634 by Duke Maximilien de Béthune, Duke of Sully (King Henry IV's minister) who spent his final years here. While the interiors are offices (home to the Centre des Monuments Nationaux) and generally closed to visitors, you can stroll through the splendid cour d'honneur and orangery garden daily. The trim hedges and citrus trees provide a glimpse of 17th-century aristocratic life. Tip: enter through Place des Vosges' southwest passage and emerge into Sully's photogenic courtyard –

it's like a secret shortcut through time, especially charming when afternoon light slants across the stone arcades.

Hôtel de Sens – 1 Rue du Figuier (Exterior and Library; limited access): A rare medieval mansion in Paris, the turreted Hôtel de Sens was built circa 1500 for the Archbishop of Sens. Its chunky towers, pointed gables, and even a lodged cannonball in the wall (from the 1830 Revolution) transport you to the Middle Ages. The building has seen drama – Marguerite de Valois (Queen Margot) lived here briefly in 1605 after her wild marriage to Henry IV, supposedly growing apricot trees in the garden and quarreling with lovers. Today it houses the Forney art library. Visitors can enter its courtyard freely and sometimes the library's exhibition hall. Notice the ornate Gothic stonework: carved coats of arms, mullioned windows, and the tiny turret with a conical witch 's-hat roof. It's one of the Marais' most picturesque sights – a little palace that predates even Notre-Dame – and a reminder that Paris' story reaches back to Renaissance bishops and rebel queens.

Hôtel Lambert – 2 Quai d'Anjou (Private; exterior view only): The crown jewel of Île Saint-Louis, Louis Le Vau designed this sumptuous 17th-century mansion and once hosted some of Paris's most glittering salons. In the 18th century, it was home to Marquis du Châtelet and her lover Voltaire, and in the 1840s, it became a headquarters of exiled Polish prince Adam Czartoryski, who threw grand balls attended by Chopin, Balzac, Delacroix, and more. Inside, artist Charles Le Brun painted the dazzling Herculean Gallery – a mini Hall of Mirrors that actually inspired Versailles' design. The mansion later passed to Baron de Rothschild, and most recently, a Qatari prince (it suffered a fire during renovations in 2013). Not open to the public, one can still admire its riverfront facade from the

Quai – a restrained classic front belying the opulence within. With its pedigree of occupants and the reputation as "the greatest house in Paris," the Hôtel Lambert remains a byword for aristocratic luxury and cultural prestige in Paris.

Hôtel de Lauzun – 17 Quai d'Anjou (City-owned; tours occasionally): Just a few doors down from Lambert, this mansion is smaller but steeped in bohemian lore. Built in 1657, it boasts gilded Baroque interiors and was later rented by eccentric aristocrats. In the 1840s, the poet Charles Baudelaire lived in an upstairs apartment here (then called Hôtel Pimodan) and wrote the first poems of Les Fleurs du Mal while residing there. He, along with writer Théophile Gautier, also hosted the infamous Club des Hashischins on-site – a circle of artists who held hashish "séances" in a grand room scented with Turkish drapes and smoke. Imagine a young Baudelaire lounging on a divan, exploring altered states that would inspire his poems. Today owned by the City of Paris, Lauzun is typically closed except for guided visits, but its myth persists. Look for its discreet portal and balcony from the Quai – behind them Baudelaire and friends once dreamed and indulged in this "intoxicated" sanctuary of art.

Jim Morrison's Apartment – 17 Rue Beautreillis (Exterior only, but there is an Airbnb in the apartment next door): On this quiet Marais side street stands the ivy-clad building where Jim Morrison, lead singer of The Doors, spent his final months incognito in 1971. The third-floor flat was where Morrison lived a bohemian Left Bank life with his girlfriend Pam Courson – until that fateful July night he was found dead in his bathtub at age 27. The official cause was heart failure (with countless lurid theories swirling since). Only the exterior is visible – a Haussmannian façade belies the rock history inside. Fans still stop by to snap photos or scrawl tributes (though the door is kept clean nowadays). A short walk away is the secluded Père Lachaise Cemetery, where Morrison's grave draws pilgrims – but this apartment is where the legend's Paris chapter ended. Stand across the street and you might feel a whisper of 1970s rock rebellion echoing in this oh-so-Parisian residence.

5th Arrondissement – Latin Quarter

Ernest Hemingway's First Paris Home – 74 Rue du Cardinal Lemoine (Exterior only): A modest walk-up in the student-filled Latin Quarter was the first Paris flat of a young Ernest Hemingway and his wife Hadley in 1922. They rented a cold-water flat here – no hot water, a shared toilet in the hall, and they slept on a mattress on the floor. Yet Hemingway later wrote that in these cramped rooms "we were very poor and very happy" (a quote you'll find on the building's plaque). This is where he began his writing career in earnest, drafting stories and hanging out at local cafes. Not open inside, but you can spot the plaque on the façade commemorating "the American writer's first Parisian home" and imagine the 22-year-old Hemingway returning here with baguettes and wine, determined to write one true sentence. The surrounding winding streets still retain the scrappy charm he described in A Moveable Feast.

Paul Verlaine's Final Abode – 39 Rue Descartes (Exterior / bar on ground floor): Tucked above what is now a typical Latin Quarter bistro was the shabby room where Paul Verlaine, the great Symbolist poet, died in 1896. By then, Verlaine was penniless, ill, and addicted to absinthe – truly living the fin-de-siècle bohemian cliché. A plaque on the wall solemnly notes: "Here died the poet Paul Verlaine". In his last years, Verlaine haunted the nearby cafés (legend has him drinking himself into stupors at the downstairs cabaret), earning the nickname "Prince of Poets" just before his death despite his destitution. Today, the ground floor is the "Caveau des Oubliettes" bar, and Verlaine's tiny attic is inaccessible. But stop on this quiet street and look up – picture Verlaine's candle casting shadows as he scribbled a few final verses. His contemporaries later rallied to give him a proper burial and memorialize this humble garret as a literary landmark.

6th Arrondissement – Saint-Germain & Luxembourg

Gertrude Stein's Salon – 27 Rue de Fleurus (Exterior only): Behind an unassuming door on this Left Bank Street was arguably the most famous artistic salon of the 1920s. American expat writer Gertrude Stein and her partner Alice B. Toklas lived here, and every Saturday evening their home became the gathering place of the "Lost Generation." Picasso, Hemingway, Matisse, Fitzgerald – all passed through Stein's cozy atelier, trading ideas beneath walls lined with Stein's radical art collection. Though not open to visitors now, a plaque marks the spot. Pause here and picture the scene Stein described: a stove burning warm, glasses of wine, and young geniuses debating art into the night. It was "perhaps the most important apartment of the 1920s from an artistic point of view," as one historian put it. The creative energy fostered here helped shape modern art and literature, all from a humble Paris flat you could easily walk past without realizing its legacy. The apartment is close to the Luxembourg Gardens, the perfect spot to stroll and contemplate the artists who walked the same pebble paths.

Oscar Wilde's Last Home (L'Hôtel) – 13 Rue des Beaux-Arts (Now a hotel & bar): In 1900, penniless and ill, Oscar Wilde took refuge in the then-seedy Hôtel d'Alsace on this quiet street – "I am dying beyond my means," he quipped of the dingy lodgings. It was here, in Room 16, that Wilde died, famously quipping about the wallpaper ("one of us has to go"). Today the place is a chic boutique L'Hôtel, and the Oscar Wilde Suite (now luxurious) bears his name. The ground-floor bar "Le Wilde's" welcomes visitors for cocktails amid velvet and jazz – a far cry from the filthy flophouse Wilde knew.

Open to the public (hotel guests or bar visitors), you can sip an absinthe cocktail in homage. After Wilde's passing, this hotel ironically hosted many celebrities (Salvador Dalí, Grace Kelly, Sinatra, etc.), but it's Wilde's witty ghost that defines it. The management embraces the legacy – a plaque and portraits remind us that here lies the great wit's tragic full stop.

Musée National Eugène Delacroix – 6 Rue de Furstenberg (Open to the public): Tucked in a picturesque courtyard off Place Furstenberg, this intimate museum was the last home and studio of Eugène Delacroix, the Romantic master painter. Delacroix moved here in 1857 to be near Saint-Sulpice (where he was painting a chapel) and lived and worked on-site until he died in 1863. Today, you can step into his preserved apartment – see his cozy bedroom and easel – then step through a glass door into the charming private garden and studio he built. The studio, with its large north-facing window, still displays Delacroix's easels, palettes, and sketches, immersing you in the ambiance of artistic creation. Open as a national museum (run by the Louvre), it's a peaceful haven where you can view Delacroix's memorabilia and works up close. Don't miss the romantic little flower garden he tended – a quiet retreat that feels miles away from the city, just as it did for Delacroix in his final years.

Musée Zadkine (Sculptor's Studio) – 100 bis Rue d'Assas: Just steps from the Luxembourg Gardens, the ivy-covered home and studio of sculptor Ossip Zadkine is a lesser-known delight. The Russian-born artist lived and worked here from 1928 until he died in 1967, and after his widow's bequest, the studio became a free museum. Tucked behind a gate, you'll find a series of studios filled with Zadkine's cubist and primitive-influenced wood and bronze sculptures, bathed in natural light. The tiny orchard-like garden is populated with his larger bronze figures – an oasis of art and greenery in the middle of Paris. Inside, rooms still have the atmosphere of a working atelier, with tools and rough-hewn blocks alongside finished pieces. Visitors are able to wander Zadkine's world. It's an off-the-beaten-path gem for design lovers, offering an "atelier visit" experience and a tangible sense of Montparnasse's creative community between the wars.

Françoise Sagan's Apartment – 34 Rue Guynemer (Exterior only): Overlooking the Luxembourg Gardens, writer Françoise Sagan (famed for Bonjour Tristesse) kept a swanky modern apartment here during her wild heyday in the 1950s–60s. Sagan moved in as a literary prodigy at age 20 and became notorious for the nonstop parties in this ultramodern flat. She even famously kept a big bowl of cash in the living room for friends to help themselves – a testament to her devil-may-care generosity. The apartment's sleek mid-century design (for its time) and floor-to-ceiling windows were the backdrop to gatherings of Paris' intellectual jeunesse dorée. Sadly, Sagan's open-handed lifestyle contributed to her later financial ruin. It's a private residence now, so one can only admire the façade facing the Jardin du Luxembourg and imagine the jazz, champagne, and cigarette smoke that once filled those rooms. This address remains a symbol of Left Bank bohemian glamour – and the hard-living "too fast to live" ethos of Françoise Sagan.

Sidenote: *Sagan Spotting in Paris*

Françoise Sagan may have written about the wild passions of the Riviera, but traces of her literary soul linger right here in Paris. You can steep yourself in her legacy at the Médiathèque Françoise Sagan in the 10th arrondissement—a serene, bookish haven housed in a restored 19th-century hospital and prison. The building is as layered as her prose, now home to exhibitions, cultural events, and a reading room that feels tailor-made for daydreamers.

Want a more intimate brush with Sagan? Head to the Hôtel de Lille, where one of the rooms is entirely dedicated to her—complete with vintage photos, curated furniture, and objects reminiscent of her stylish, cigarette-smoke-and-literature lifestyle.

And if you wander near Maxim's, you might just feel the echo of her wit from the days Bonjour Tristesse made her a sensation. In Paris, some legacies don't need plaques—they hang in the air.

7th Arrondissement – Faubourg Saint-Germain & Eiffel Tower

Musée Rodin (Hôtel Biron) – 77 Rue de Varenne (Open to the public): The Hôtel Biron is an exquisite 1732 rococo mansion set in a formal garden – a serene backdrop for the brooding bronzes of Auguste Rodin. Rodin discovered this dilapidated gem in 1908 when it was "practically abandoned" and rented rooms as his studio. By 1911, he had taken over the entire mansion and its grounds, filling it with marble and plaster as he sculpted. Rodin later donated all his works to the state on condition that they turn Hôtel Biron into a museum. Today, you can wander the Musée Rodin and see The Kiss and The Thinker bathed in natural light in what were once Rodin's workspaces. The elegant wood-paneled salons and grand staircase provide a fitting "18th-century mansion" setting for his art. Outside, the rose gardens and lily ponds are dotted with sculptures (spot The Thinker pondering among the hedges). Open to visitors, this museum is a magical blend of art and place, as Rodin himself chose and designed it – truly "an extraordinary harmony" of setting and sculpture.

Hôtel Matignon (Prime Minister's Residence) – 57 Rue de Varenne (Closed to the public except heritage days): A grand 18th-century mansion set behind high walls and a huge private park, Hôtel de Matignon has been the official residence of France's Prime Ministers since 1935. It was built in 1722–1725 by architect Jean Courtonne for the Prince of Monaco, and its sumptuous interiors and 3-hectare garden quickly became legendary. The Matignon garden is, in fact, the largest private garden in Paris – approximately 2 hectares of manicured lawn, allées of linden trees, and even a vegetable patch for the chefs. While not open to daily visits, Matignon opens on rare occasions (European Heritage Weekend) when the public queues for a peek at the mirrored Salle à Manger and the Salon Bleu, where heads of state have chatted. *Fun fact:* General de Gaulle reportedly loved strolling these very grounds. If you walk by on Rue de Varenne, all you'll see is the regal gate and guard post – but know that behind them lies an estate of glittering reception rooms and an "outstanding" park that few get to see.

Maison de Serge Gainsbourg – 5 bis Rue de Verneuil (Museum – guided visits by reservation): For years, fans of provocative singer Serge Gainsbourg have flocked to this ivy-draped townhouse in Saint-Germain, covering its street wall with colorful graffiti tributes. Gainsbourg lived here from 1969 until his death in 1991, writing hits in its smoky rooms and famously sharing the space with English muse Jane Birkin for a time. In 2023, the house finally opened as Maison Gainsbourg, a museum where visitors (in small guided groups) can step inside Serge's world. The interior has been preserved exactly as he left it – the eclectic art, the piano, overflowing ashtrays, and his legendary collection of exotic tchotchkes. Touring it feels like entering a 1970s time capsule of Parisian rock-bohemia. Outside, the frontage remains plastered in fan graffiti and poems, a living shrine to French pop culture's enfant terrible. Open by advance booking only (visit the official website for tickets, MaisonGainsbourg.com), Maison Gainsbourg offers an intimate, quirky, and very special peek into the life of a legend, completing the transformation of this address from a private lair to a national monument of chanson.

Sidenote: *The Birkin Bag Was Born on a Barf Bag*

Only in Paris could elegance spring from turbulence—literally. In the 1980s, actress and style icon Jane Birkin (Muse of Serge) boarded a flight from Paris to London with a straw tote bursting at the seams (as any stylish over-packer knows). As fate would have it, her seatmate was none other than Jean-Louis Dumas, Executive Chairman of Hermès.

When the contents of her bag tumbled into the aisle mid-flight, Birkin casually complained that no bag on the market seemed to fit her glamorous-yet-practical needs. Dumas, ever the gentleman-designer, handed her an airplane sick bag and said, "Sketch it."

She did. Right then and there. And from that crumpled little vomit bag came the most coveted handbag of all time: the Birkin. Proof that sometimes, luxury begins with a mess and a good listener.

Hôtel de Beauharnais (German Ambassador's Residence) – 78 Rue de Lille (Closed to the public except special events): Tucked behind a high wall is a mansion with one of Paris's most opulent Empire-style interiors. Built in 1714 by architect Germain Boffrand, it was later purchased in 1803 by Prince Eugène de Beauharnais (Napoleon's stepson). Eugène lavishly redecorated it in full Napoleonic glamour: gilded swan motifs, sphinxes, mahogany furniture, and Egyptian Revival touches commemorate Napoleon's campaigns. The result – Hôtel de Beauharnais – remains perhaps the best-preserved Consulate/Empire décor in France. Today, it serves as the official residence of the German Ambassador (Germany's elegant foothold in Paris since 1968). The French have classified their salons as historic monuments – indeed, stepping inside is like walking into 1805, with rooms still set as if Josephine might waltz in at any moment. Generally closed (though occasionally opened for guided tours or heritage days), one can only admire the dignified Neoclassical façade on Rue de Lille and imagine the treasures within. It's a hidden Napoleonic gem that illustrates the peak of Imperial luxury, all behind closed doors of diplomacy. Check out the official website for entry details.

Julia Child's Apartment ("Roo de Loo") – 81 Rue de l'Université (Exterior only): On a chic street near the Musée d'Orsay, the top floors of No.81 were home to American chef Julia Child and her husband Paul during her transformative Paris years (1948–1953). Julia affectionately dubbed the street "Roo de Loo" for short. In this roomy, oddly laid-out apartment (since divided into condos), Julia mastered French cooking, notably honing recipes for Mastering the Art of French Cooking. She famously had to improvise because the counters were too low for her 6'2" frame! This is where she experimented with boeuf bourguignon and potage parmentier, filling the place with delicious aromas and occasional smoke. The apartment is private, but fans often stop to snap a photo of the unassuming stone façade. You can almost picture Julia leaning out the window (as in a famous photo) with a copper saucepan in hand. For foodies, this address is hallowed ground – the very spot where Julia Child's passion for French cuisine took flight, changing how Americans cook forever.

Sidenote: *Cocktails and Culinary Legends*

When Julia and Paul Child first touched down in Paris in November 1948, they didn't just fall in love with the city—they moved right into its literary heart. Their temporary home? The elegant Hotel Pont Royal, tucked away in the refined 7th arrondissement.

This hotel isn't just a pretty place to stay—it's a piece of Parisian cultural history. Its cozy Bar Signature was reportedly the first real cocktail bar to open in the city between the World Wars, and it quickly became a magnet for creative greats. Imagine the conversations swirling between sips, as legends like Hemingway, Simone de Beauvoir, and the Fitzgeralds unwound in leather club chairs.

Julia, never one to shy away from flavor, was said to favor an Upside-Down Martini. If you're in the mood for a little time travel, settle into a corner of that warm, wood-paneled bar and raise a glass to the woman who brought French cooking into American kitchens—with a whole lot of style.

Hotel Pont Royal

5–7 Rue de Montalembert, 75007 Paris

Nearest Metro: Rue du Bac (Line 12)

8th Arrondissement – Champs-Élysées & Monceau

Musée Jacquemart-André – 158 Boulevard Haussmann (Open to public): Once a private mansion of affluent art collectors Edouard André and Nélie Jacquemart, this Belle Époque palace (built 1875) now invites the public to relive the splendor of the 19th-century high society. It's perfectly preserved state rooms – including a grand double-helix marble staircase adorned with a Giambattista Tiepolo ceiling fresco – exude pure extravagance. Visiting feels like attending a gala in 1880: you wander through a Winter Garden of exotic plants under a glass roof, a Music Room with gilded panels, and a dining room hung with Italian Renaissance paintings. The collection is as impressive as the setting, featuring Rembrandts, Botticellis, fragonard panels – the "finest private collection of art works in Paris" at one time. Open as a museum, Jacquemart-André lets you time-travel to the days of waltzes and wainscoting. Don't skip tea in the lavish salon turned café, where you can sip under cherub-painted ceilings as if you're a guest of the Andrées.

Musée Nissim de Camondo – 63 Rue de Monceau (Open to public): Overlooking Parc Monceau, the Camondo mansion was purpose-built in 1911–14 to house one man's incredible collection of 18th-century French decorative arts. Count Moïse de Camondo, from a wealthy Sephardic Jewish banking family, modeled this home after Versailles' Petit Trianon – complete with an elegant, curved exterior and perfectly symmetrical salons. Inside, it's a treasure trove of Louis XVI furniture, Sèvres porcelain, and Aubusson tapestries. You'll see Marie-Antoinette's hand-painted porcelains and furniture by master cabinetmakers (like Riesener and Oeben) in rooms lit by crystal chandeliers. Yet a poignant history underlies the beauty: Moïse bequeathed the house as a museum in 1935 in memory of his son Nissim, killed in WWI– and later his daughter Béatrice and her children perished in Auschwitz. The result is a house museum frozen in time. Open to visitors, it offers an unmatched "panorama of 18th-century art". Walk through the dining room set for an aristocratic dinner and the pristine kitchens, and you'll feel the glories and sorrows of a vanished era entwined in this spectacular home.

Élysée Palace – 55 Rue du Faubourg Saint-Honoré (Not open, except rare events): The Palais de l'Élysée is France's version of the White House – the official residence and office of the President. Completed in 1722 for the Count of Évreux, it later hosted Madame de Pompadour (mistress of Louis XV) and even Napoleon Bonaparte himself. The mansion's dignified classical facade hides a labyrinth of sumptuous state rooms in varying historical styles (from the gold-and-mirror Salle des Fêtes ballroom to Napoleon III's lavish private theater). Out back lies a magnificent 2-hectare garden – a rarity in central Paris – where presidents host garden parties and where Emmanuel and Brigitte Macron can stroll among hundred-year-old trees. The Élysée is heavily guarded and closed to daily visits, but every September on Heritage Days a lucky few gain entry, lining up for hours to see the Salon d'Argent and the President's desk. On an ordinary day, you can only peer through the iron gates on Rue du Fbg St-Honoré to glimpse the Cour d'Honneur where visiting heads of state arrive. This address is the pinnacle of French power – 300 years of history sealed behind those gates, yet firmly at the heart of the nation's story.

Sidenote: *Mistresses, Cake, and a Vegetable Patch—Oh My!*

The Élysée Palace may be the seat of presidential power today, but don't let its stately exterior fool you—it's seen its fair share of drama, decadence, and a few unexpected garden vegetables.

Before it became the French president's official residence, the palace moonlighted as a full-fledged "pleasure palace" during the French Directory era (yes, really). And when Napoleon III moved in, he added his own twist: a "secret" tunnel connecting the palace chapel to a nearby townhouse—conveniently located for discreet late-night visits to his mistresses. Très subtle.

Even its origins are humble. The land was once a vegetable patch, part of the then-rural Faubourg-du-Roule neighborhood. Today, it's surrounded by Parisian splendor—Rue du Faubourg Saint-Honoré is now lined with couture houses, embassies, and polished government buildings.

And in case you were wondering, even dessert here comes with political restraint. During Epiphany, the palace serves a bean-free Galette des Rois—because symbolically crowning the president as king? That would be a faux pas of revolutionary proportions.

As for the palace's posh neighbors? A stroll down Rue du Faubourg Saint-Honoré will take you past haute couture houses, embassies, and the Ministry of the Interior itself. You know, just in case you're shopping for a handbag and state secrets in the same afternoon.

Hôtel de la Païva – 25 Avenue des Champs-Élysées (Private club; occasional tours): Along the Champs-Élysées stands a mansion born of scandal and extravagance – built between 1856 and 1866 for La Païva, one of Paris's most famous courtesans. Arriving from humble beginnings, La Païva vowed to "have the most beautiful house on the

Champs-Élysées" – and she did. Inside, her home is a riot of Second Empire opulence: a bright yellow Algerian onyx staircase spirals up from the foyer, one-of-a-kind in the world. Sumptuous frescoes by Paul Baudry (painter of the Opera Garnier) adorn the ceilings, and mythological sculptures by young Auguste Rodin ornament the walls. In the Moorish-style bathroom, an onyx bathtub with gold-plated taps reputedly allowed her to bathe in milk, champagne, or perfumed water at will. La Païva hosted lavish literary salons here, entertaining the likes of Goncourt, Gautier, and Offenbach under gilded chandeliers. Today, the mansion is home to a private gentlemen's club (Travellers Club) closed to casual visitors. But occasionally it offers guided tours, where one can gasp at the preserved splendor – from the balustrades wrought like wrought-iron seahorses to the Gaudí-esque glass dome. It's an ancien-régime-meets-Belle-Époque fantasy come true, and a monument to how one extraordinary woman bent Paris to her dreams.

9th Arrondissement – Nouvelle Athènes & Opéra

Musée de la Vie Romantique – 16 Rue Chaptal (Open to public): Down a tree-shaded lane, a green-shuttered villa reveals the intimate world of the Romantic era. This was the home and studio of painter Ary Scheffer in the 1830s–40s, where every Friday he hosted salons frequented by the likes of George Sand, Frédéric Chopin, Eugène Delacroix, and other Romantic luminaries. Today it's the Museum of Romantic Life, and as you step through the courtyard gate, time slips backwards. Inside the cozy rooms, you'll find Sand's personal jewelry, miniature portraits, and even her love letters; on the walls hang Scheffer's dreamy paintings and those of his contemporaries. The creaky floorboards and flowered wallpaper set a suitably sentimental tone. Open to visitors (free entry), the museum also offers a delightful garden café among rose bushes – perfect for daydreaming with a cup of tea. It's easy to imagine Chopin's music drifting through the open windows or Sand sweeping in wearing a man's suit. A visit here truly "transports visitors back to 19th-century Paris," into a haven of art, music, and romantic intrigue.

Square d'Orléans – 80 Rue Taitbout (Private courtyard; view through gate): Hidden behind a carriage gate on rue Taitbout lies Square d'Orléans, a lovely private courtyard complex that was once nicknamed "The Citadel of Art". In the 1840s, this elegant Neoclassical square became a residence for artists, most famously George Sand and Frédéric Chopin. The writer and composer carried on their love affair here, living in separate apartments that faced one another across the courtyard (Sand at No.5, Chopin at No.9). Imagine Chopin composing at his piano while Sand scribbles at her desk next door! The great dancer Marie

Taglioni also resided here, as did painter Ary Scheffer's brother. Today, it remains a private gated residence (it's said that fashion designer Pierre Cardin once had a flat here, too). You can't enter without an invitation, but you can peek through the iron gate at the tranquil courtyard with its central fountain. It's lined by creamy Classical facades with columned porticos – like a little slice of Regency London in Paris. A plaque notes Chopin and Sand's stay. In its heyday (1842–47), "both lived there from 1842 till 1847, the year of the big breakup"– their romance echoed by the serene symmetry of the square. It's a romantic pilgrimage spot, even if seen only from the outside.

Musée Gustave Moreau – 14 Rue de La Rochefoucauld (Open to the public): Gustave Moreau, the Symbolist painter, turned his family home into a fantastical museum of his life's work – and it's one of Paris's most enchanting artist house-museums. Tucked on a quiet street near Pigalle, the museum still feels like Moreau just stepped out for a moment. Downstairs, you wander through his cozy former apartment, with plush furniture and trinkets from his travels. But the showstopper is upstairs: two grand, sky-lit studio floors where hundreds of Moreau's mystical, dreamlike paintings cover the walls from floor to ceiling. Nude goddesses, chimera, and biblical scenes crowd the space in a sort of deliberately "uninhibited disarray" of a painter's atelier. Connecting the studios is an iconic spiral staircase of wood and wrought iron – a graceful helix often likened to an Art Nouveau sculpture itself. Moreau designed this staircase in 1896 when preparing the museum, ensuring visitors could drift effortlessly between his two levels of paintings. Open to the public, the museum has scarcely changed since it opened in 1903. It's an immersive portal into Moreau's psyche – as you climb that spiral stair, surrounded by vibrant canvases of mythical beasts, you truly feel the "sensitive and honest" atmosphere Moreau intended for each room.

11th Arrondissement – Ménilmontant & Oberkampf

Musée Édith Piaf – 5 Rue Crespin-du-Gast (Open by appointment, free): In a nondescript 4th-floor apartment of the 11th lies a tiny two-room museum dedicated to Édith Piaf, France's beloved chanteuse. This was the actual little flat where Piaf lived in 1933 at the dawn of her career, and a devout fan has turned it into a shrine filled with her personal items. Stepping inside (by prior arrangement – ring the bell for "Les Amis de Piaf"), you're greeted by a life-sized photo of "la Môme Piaf" and cabinets crammed with memorabilia: sparkling stage dresses, towering heels, handwritten letters, gold records, and even her teddy bear and makeup kit. Fading photos of Piaf with lovers and friends cover the walls. It feels more like visiting your eccentric aunt's parlor than a formal museum – wonderfully intimate and heartfelt. The space is maintained by a private collector who might regale you with Piaf anecdotes. Admission is free (donations welcome) but must be reserved, and the experience is delightfully uncommercial. As you stand in the very room where young Édith sang a cappella for friends, it's easy to imagine her voice echoing off these walls. A truly special stop for any music lover wanting to get close, physically and emotionally, to the "Little Sparrow" of France.

13th Arrondissement – Modernist Landmarks

Maison Planeix – 24 bis Boulevard Masséna (Exterior only): Amid the high-rises and périphérique of south Paris stands an early modernist gem by Le Corbusier. The narrow white Planeix House, built in 1928 for sculptor Antonin Planeix, looks strikingly contemporary with its clean lines and ribbon windows. Perched on thin "pilotis" columns that lift it above street level, it embodied Corbu's radical ideas in a domestic building. This was one of Le Corbusier's few realized private houses within Paris, and its functional, cube-like design (with a roof terrace and minimalist façade) scandalized neighbors accustomed to more ornate styles. Today, it's flanked by later buildings, but it still "stands out amidst the surrounding cityscape for its refined simplicity. It's a private residence (divided into apartments), so one can only view it from Boulevard Masséna. But architecture buffs often make a detour to see the trademark features: ground-floor studios with glass brick, horizontal strip windows on upper floors, and the stark geometry that forecast the International Style. Consider it a drive-by pilgrimage – a small but significant chapter in modern architecture history tucked in an unlikely corner of the 13th.

Sidenote: *Pho, Frescoes, and the Future of Paris*

The 13th arrondissement may not drip with romantic clichés or gilded façades, but it's got attitude, art, and some serious surprises. Once a largely industrial zone, this neighborhood has evolved into a hub of bold creativity—with just enough grit to keep things interesting.

Start with the towering murals that make the district feel like an open-air museum. International street artists—from Obey (Shepard Fairey) to Invader—have splashed their visions across entire building façades, creating one of the largest concentrations of street art in Europe. Forget quiet gallery walks; here, you crane your neck and let the walls do the storytelling.

If brutalist architecture makes your heart flutter (don't worry, you're among friends), stop by the Bibliothèque François Mitterrand, a strikingly modern national library made up of four glass towers shaped like open books. Whether you're inside browsing rare volumes or outside admiring its reflective symmetry, it feels more sci-fi than classical Paris—but in the best way.

And yes, you absolutely can—and should—stop for pho. The area's large Vietnamese and Laotian communities mean you're never far from an excellent bowl of broth and noodles. Rue de Tolbiac and Avenue d'Ivry are local go-tos, and honestly? There's something deeply satisfying about sipping steamy soup in the same arrondissement where concrete modernism and colossal graffiti reign supreme.

Because Paris isn't just a postcard—it's a patchwork. And the 13th? That's where it gets delightfully off-script.

- Boulevard Vincent Auriol: Home to massive murals by Shepard Fairey, C215, and Invader. Bring your camera.

- Rue Jeanne d'Arc & Rue Esquirol: Unexpected masterpieces tucked between apartment blocks.

- Bibliothèque François Mitterrand

- Quirky modernist icon made of four giant glass towers shaped like open books.

- Quai François Mauriac, 75013 – Metro: Bibliothèque François Mitterrand (Line 14)

- Pho Banh Cuon 14 – Local favorite for steaming, aromatic broth.

- 129 Avenue de Choisy – Metro: Tolbiac or Olympiades

- Hao Hao – No-frills, big flavor. Go for the Bun Bo Hue.

- 188 Avenue de Choisy – Metro: Porte de Choisy

14th Arrondissment: Montparnasse & Montsouris

Villa Seurat Artists' Colony – Villa Seurat (Exterior only): On a tiny impasse off Rue de la Tombe-Issoire lies Villa Seurat, a private cul-de-sac of modernist houses that in the late 1920s formed a bohemian enclave. The street (named after painter Georges Seurat) was developed by architect André Lurçat between 1924–1926 as live-in studios for artists. Here, every house has a creative pedigree: No.7 was home to sculptor Chana Orloff (in a cubist studio by Auguste Perret, complete with red doors and a historic turret-like stair); No.11 hosted sculptor Arnold Huggler; and most famously, Henry Miller lived at No.18 in the 1930s. Miller rented a studio-bedroom in 1934 (from writer Michael Fraenkel) and finished Tropic of Cancer here – calling Villa Seurat "the whole street is given up to quiet joyous work... every house contains a writer, painter, musician, sculptor or actor..." During WWII, painter Chaïm Soutine also hid out briefly at No. 18. Today, Villa Seurat remains a leafy gated lane. It's residential and private, but a peek from the entrance reveals clean white façades, glass-brick ateliers, and the distinctive porthole windows and curved walls of Lurçat's design. Villa Seurat encapsulates that 1920s ideal of "a sensitive and honest" modern architecture tailored to artists' lives– a tiny time capsule of avant-garde Montparnasse.

15th Arrondissement – Montparnasse's Legacy

La Ruche ("The Beehive" Artists' Colony) – 2 Passage Dantzig (Exterior courtyard; sometimes open during events): Down a quiet alley in the 15th stands an eccentric round building known as La Ruche – once a legendary hive of artists. This three-story circular structure (originally built by Gustave Eiffel as a wine rotunda for the 1900 World's Fair) was moved here in 1902 and converted into cheap studios. By the 1910s–20s, it hosted a who's who of emerging artists: Marc Chagall, Fernand Léger, Chaïm Soutine, Amedeo Modigliani, Osip Zadkine, and poet Blaise Cendrars all worked (and struggled) here. The accommodations were Spartan – partitioned wood cubicles with no heat or running water, likened to a "maze-like conglomerate" that creaked in the wind like a river barge. The name "La Ruche" (beehive) stuck for its buzzing creative energy and cylindrical shape. Many a modern art masterpiece was conceived under its leaky roof – Chagall painted scenes of Russia here, and legends say rent was sometimes paid in paintings. Over time, the colony fell into disrepair (and nearly demolition), but it still stands, refurbished and still housing about 50 working artist studios today. While not regularly open to tourists, you can enter the Passage Dantzig to view the distinctive round structure and perhaps catch an open studio day. It remains a "symbol of Art Nouveau in Paris", an enduring bohemian landmark where the ghosts of starving artists past continue to inspire.

Musée Bourdelle – 18 Rue Antoine Bourdelle (Open to the public, free): Tucked behind Montparnasse Tower's bustle lies a secret garden-atelier that transports you to the age of Rodin and Claudel.

This was the home and studio of sculptor Antoine Bourdelle, a pupil of Rodin and a master in his own right. The museum encompasses Bourdelle's original 19th-century studios – brick industrial-style halls with enormous windows – as well as peaceful courtyard gardens where his monumental bronzes stand amid ivy and rosebushes. Inside, the Great Hall is lined with heroically sized plaster casts and marbles (Bourdelle specialized in muscular, mythic figures). You'll see his famous "Hercules the Archer" poised mid-shot in the garden, and in his preserved studio space, you can almost sense the artist at work – tools and unfinished clay pieces lying about, dust motes in the sunlight. Admission is free, making it a delightful escape. The mix of art and atmosphere is noteworthy: "the museum preserves the studio...providing an example of Parisian ateliers from the late 19th and early 20th centuries". It's a hidden haven where you can wander at leisure, often nearly alone with the sculptures – a romantic, slightly melancholic reminder of Montparnasse's artistic golden days.

16th Arrondissement – Passy & Auteuil

Maison de Balzac – 47 Rue Raynouard (Open as a museum, free): In a leafy corner of Passy sits a modest ivy-covered house where Honoré de Balzac hid from creditors under an assumed name. From 1840 to 1847, Balzac rented rooms here, using the alias "Brugnon" as he toiled on La Comédie Humaine. Today it's the Balzac Museum, and stepping inside, you find walls lined with the author's portraits, manuscripts, and cherished objects. Balzac's writing desk and chair are on display, as are first editions of his novels and even his personal coffee pot (he infamously fueled himself with dozens of cups a day). The house's highlight is its garden – unexpectedly large for Paris – which slopes down with a postcard view of the Eiffel Tower in the distance. You can sit under the arbor where Balzac once pondered characters and feel the quiet that belies the city around. Admission is free to this cozy literary shrine. Don't miss the underground storeroom – Balzac had an escape tunnel through it to Rue Berton in case bailiffs came knocking! In this humble retreat, the great realist crafted his vast fictional world, and visiting feels like dropping in on a hardworking friend (with a genius imagination) in his down-to-earth home.

Musée Marmottan Monet – 2 Rue Louis Boilly (Open to public): Originally a hunting lodge turned elegant mansion owned by collector Paul Marmottan, this museum is a temple to Impressionism tucked next to the Ranelagh gardens. The mansion retains its perfectly preserved Empire-style decor – glittering chandeliers, silk-covered walls, and a grand Napoleon III library. But descend to the special exhibition gallery and you'll find the world's largest collection of Monets displayed in an intimate setting. Over 100 of Claude

Monet's works are here, from his early Argenteuil landscapes to multiple panels of the Water Lilies that turn the walls into a panorama of Giverny's pond. It was at Marmottan that Impression, Sunrise – the painting that gave Impressionism its name – found its home, donated by Monet's son. The collection also boasts the largest ensemble of works by female Impressionist Berthe Morisot. Wandering the galleries, you experience an almost private dialogue with these masterpieces, far from the crowds of larger museums. Open to visitors, Marmottan Monet offers a unique dual charm: upstairs, you wander through opulent salons with Sèvres vases and medieval illuminations, and downstairs, you are immersed in the luminous haze of Monet's world. It truly "offers a unique experience of his art in terms of both quantity and rarity"– a hidden jewel in a quiet upscale neighborhood.

Villa La Roche (Le Corbusier Foundation) – 8-10 Square du Docteur Blanche (Open to the public): In a small cul-de-sac of Auteuil stands a stark white villa that is a pilgrimage site for architecture students worldwide – Maison La Roche, designed by Le Corbusier in 1923. Built as a combined gallery-home for collector Raoul La Roche and an adjacent residence for Le Corbusier's brother, this twin villa complex embodies the "Five Points" of modern architecture: pilotis columns, a functional roof terrace, an open plan, horizontal ribbon windows, and a free façade. Inside, visitors can follow a swooping promenade architecturale up a curved ramp and staircase, through double-height volumes and oddly shaped rooms precisely calibrated for displaying Cubist art. The color scheme – pale rose, celadon green, white – is restored to 1920s purist taste. The villa is now the Le Corbusier Foundation HQ and museum, so open for tours, allowing you to walk on the mezzanine and peer down into the atrium just as

Corbu intended. It's fascinating to compare the compact living quarters (a tiny kitchen and bachelor bedroom) with the dramatic gallery space lit by a high skylight. The feeling is of being in a three-dimensional Mondrian painting. Outside, the villa's façade is an asymmetric collage of rectangles and projecting balconies – still strikingly contemporary. Tucked in a leafy private court, it's a calm, almost reverential site. For design enthusiasts, this is not just a house, but a manifesto in concrete and glass, offering a chance to literally walk through the blueprint of modern living.

Castel Béranger – 14 Rue La Fontaine (Exterior only): In the wealthy streets of Auteuil stands Castel Béranger, an apartment building that in 1898 heralded the Art Nouveau movement in Paris. Architect Hector Guimard (famed for his Metro entrances) unleashed his imagination on this residence, and the result was so avant-garde, it won the city's first prize for façade beauty even as critics dubbed it "Castel Dérangé" (Crazy Castle) for its wild style. The façade is a playful mix of materials – orange brick, rough stone, glazed tiles, and wrought iron – all composed in undulating organic forms. Seahorse motifs climb the wrought-iron railings, and a fantastical, asymmetrical arch crowns the entry door. When new, this building shocked the staid 16th arrondissement, violating every Haussmannian rule – Parisians either loved it or called its young architect mad. Today it's a protected landmark and a symbol of Art Nouveau in Paris. It's private apartments, so one can only admire from the street, but that is plenty: note the sinuous carved wood door (like something from Gaudí's Barcelona) and the delicate floral patterns in the stonework. Castel Béranger turned an ordinary middle-class dwelling into a total work of art, making every passerby stop, stare, and perhaps smile at Guimard's audacity. Over a century later, it still hasn't lost its power to delight and surprise.

17th Arrondissement – Monceau & Batignolles

Hôtel Gaillard (Cité de l'Économie) – 1 Place du Général-Catroux (Open as museum): If you didn't know better, you'd think a Loire Valley château had been plopped down in northwest Paris – **that's** Hôtel Gaillard, a Neo-Renaissance fantasy built in 1882 for banker Émile Gaillard. Gaillard, a passionate collector of medieval art, spared no expense: the façade bristles with turrets, spires, and sculpted griffins, and inside were grand halls inspired by French Renaissance castles (think carved wood ceilings, monumental fireplaces, stained glass). After Gaillard's death, the Banque de France took it over – its most beautiful branch office, complete with a cavernous vault room protected by a moat and drawbridge! Now, after meticulous restoration, this architectural gem is reborn as Citéco – the Museum of Economics, so the public can finally enter. Visitors can ogle the lavish historic rooms (fully listed as Monuments) while engaging with interactive exhibits about money and markets. Highlights include the former bank vault, lined floor-to-ceiling with thousands of metal safe boxes – a dramatic sight – and the rooftop terrace where you can admire, up close, the ornate stone dormers and chimneys. Hôtel Gaillard's journey – from private palace to bank to museum – means its doors are now open wide. Whether you're into economics or just want to feel like royalty for a day, exploring this "neo-Renaissance architectural gem" is a visual feast. It's not often you learn about supply and demand under gilded candelabras and painted coats-of-arms!

18th Arrondissement – Montmartre

Dalida's House – 11 bis Rue d'Orchampt (Exterior only): In a secluded lane atop Montmartre sits the former home of singer Dalida, one of France's most idolized divas. She moved into this elegant three-story villa in 1962 and lived here until her untimely death in 1987. The house, now partitioned into private apartments, still exudes quiet luxury – white façade, green shutters, and a small garden, with (as Dalida enjoyed) a splendid view over Paris, including the Eiffel Tower from the upper floors. A plaque by the gate reads: "Dalida lived in this house from 1962–1987 – her Montmartre friends will never forget her." Fans often pause here on their way to the nearby Place Dalida (where her bronze bust stands) to leave flowers or simply pay respects. Though not open inside, the villa's presence on this peaceful street, a stone's throw from the Moulin de la Galette, evokes the star's deep connection to Montmartre. She was known to stroll these very streets like a neighborhood local. The surrounding area remains much as she adored: village-like calm, ivy-clad walls, and artistic spirit. Standing at her gate, you can almost hear the distant echo of "Je suis malade" drifting on the breeze – an homage to the enduring bond between Dalida and Montmartre.

Le Bateau-Lavoir – 13 Rue Ravignan (Place Émile-Goudeau) (Exterior, courtyard occasionally open): This unassuming site was the crucible of modern art – a dilapidated wooden studio complex nicknamed "Le Bateau-Lavoir" because it creaked like a Seine laundry barge in the wind. In 1904, a young Pablo Picasso rented a studio here for 5 francs a month. Over the next few years, this warren of 20+ artist studios housed an astonishing roster of avant-garde talent: Picasso painted his revolutionary Les Demoiselles d'Avignon here in

1907; Amedeo Modigliani, Juan Gris, and Kees van Dongen lived and worked here; writers like Guillaume Apollinaire and Max Jacob hung about; even early performances of African tribal dancers occurred in the courtyards, influencing the artists. It was cramped, dirty, and freezing – "a confusing warren of corridors, creaking stairs, groaning floorboards and damp walls," as one account described. A fire in 1970 destroyed the original structure (today's building is a reconstruction housing city studios), but a plaque marks its importance. The courtyard is normally closed (sometimes opened for art events), but you can stand in front of the black wood facade on Place Émile-Goudeau and read the plaque listing Picasso & Co. This humble spot truly is where 20th-century art was born – you can practically feel the creative ghosts swirling. Pause and imagine the clamor of brushes, poets, and wild debates echoing from those windows when Montmartre was the throbbing heart of the avant-garde.

Musée de Montmartre & Renoir Gardens – 12–14 Rue Cortot (Open to public): A visit here is like walking onto an Impressionist canvas. The museum is housed in Montmartre's oldest buildings – a 17th-century manor and an 18th-century house – which themselves hosted artists Pierre-Auguste Renoir, Suzanne Valadon, and Maurice Utrillo as residents. Renoir rented a studio here in 1875; in the garden, he painted La Balançoire (The Swing) and the famous Bal du Moulin de la Galette with lively dance scenes. A century later, Valadon (one of the few celebrated female artists of her time) and her son Utrillo lived upstairs; the museum has re-created Valadon's bohemian studio exactly as it was, with paint-splattered furniture and her easel. The collections inside celebrate Montmartre's rich artistic and cabaret history – Toulouse-Lautrec posters from the Moulin

Rouge, shadow puppets from the Chat Noir cabaret, Picasso sketches, and vintage can-can costumes. But perhaps the biggest delight is outside in the Renoir Gardens: three whimsical gardens on a slope, dotted with flowers, a trellis swing (yes, like in Renoir's painting), and spectacular views of Montmartre's last vineyard and the northern city. It's easy to imagine Renoir setting up his easel amid these rose bushes. Open to visitors, the museum provides a "giddy glimpse of Montmartre life during the Belle Époque". From the quaint cafe overlooking the Clos Montmartre vines, you can sip wine where Valadon once sipped hers, and feel the artistic soul of Montmartre living on.

Vincent van Gogh's Montmartre Apartment – 54 Rue Lepic (Exterior only): On bustling Rue Lepic, above a boulangerie, a small plaque marks where Vincent van Gogh lived with his brother Theo from 1886 to 1888. In this third-floor flat, the Dutch painter, then unknown and penniless, absorbed the avant-garde ideas of Paris. He befriended Toulouse-Lautrec and Émile Bernard, traded paintings with Gauguin, and painted feverishly – scenes of Montmartre's windmills, still-lifes of flowers, view of Paris rooftops (one canvas, View from Theo's Apartment, directly depicts what he saw from this window). Those two years on Lepic were transformative: Vincent arrived painting dark, earthy tones and left for Arles having embraced the bright palette of Impressionism. The apartment itself was humble but decently sized for the brothers, and one can imagine Vincent standing by the window, looking onto the lively market street below, perhaps sketching the Moulin de la Galette visible up the hill. The building is private, but fans often pause by the doorway (next to today's bakery) and glance up, reflecting on Vincent's Paris chapter. It was here that one of history's greatest artists lived "very quietly" yet emerged ready to revolutionize art. In a city filled with grand sites, this unremarkable building reminds us that genius often germinates in the most ordinary places – a small Montmartre flat where Vincent van Gogh's world went from brown to sunflower-yellow.

Tristan Tzara House – 15 Avenue Junot (Exterior only): Amid Montmartre's quaint villas, the stark white cubist façade of the Tristan Tzara House stands out like a declaration of rebellion. This modern home, designed in 1926 by the famed Austrian architect Adolf Loos, was built for Tristan Tzara, the co-founder of the radical Dada art movement. At a time when Montmartre was mostly charming cottages, Loos delivered a flat-roofed, geometric building with strip windows and no superfluous ornament – essentially "minimalist architecture for a Dadaist". Locals were aghast, but avant-garde circles were thrilled. Tzara hosted salons here that drew Surrealists and writers; one can picture André Breton climbing the steps to discuss anti-art manifestos in Tzara's chic living room. The house itself exemplified Loos's Raumplan concept: each room a different height and volume tailored to its function, creating a dynamic interior. Though private today (divided into apartments), from the street you can admire its refined design – the perfectly balanced asymmetry, the play of shadows on the pure surfaces. A historic plaque notes its significance as Loos's only work in France. For architecture buffs, it's a must-see pilgrimage (even Forbes recently featured an apartment for sale inside, praising the "glamorous interior with brass accents"). For others, it's simply intriguing to see how the spirit of Dada – subverting norms – lives on in bricks and mortar, on a quiet Montmartre Avenue where one house unapologetically "stands out amidst the surrounding buildings for its refined design and simple lines".

Sidebar: *Montmartre Sips & Bites That Actually Deliver*

Whether you're craving artisanal coffee, scenic sips, or a memorable meal, Montmartre has you covered. Here are five standout venues— truly worth a visit:

1. **Sylon**

   A cozy local favorite serving specialty brews and freshly baked treats. Great brunch too.

   4bis Rue Piémontesi, 75018 Paris · *Metro: Abbesses (Line 12)*

2. **La Main Noire**

   A stylish spot blending street-art vibes with high-quality coffee and wholesome plates.

   12 Rue Cavallotti, 75018 Paris · *Metro: Lamarck–Caulaincourt*

3. **Les Cinq Marches**

   Tucked off the beaten path, this charming café offers organic bites and a calm, local atmosphere.

   12 Rue Girardon, 75018 Paris · *Metro: Lamarck–Caulaincourt*

4. **Café des 2 Moulins**

   The cult classic café from *Amélie*, perfect for a nostalgic coffee or light meal—with authentic Montmartre charm.

   15 Rue Lepic, 75018 Paris · *Metro: Blanche (Line 2)*

5. Le Bar à Bulles

Hidden behind Moulin Rouge, this upbeat rooftop bar offers natural wines, shareable plates, and a leafy terrace.

4 Cité Véron, 75018 Paris · *Metro: Blanche (Line 2)*

Each of these places invites you into a different story in the city's grand narrative – from medieval alchemists to Belle Époque salons, from revolutionary ateliers to rock-star hideaways. Paris's houses and residences are as varied and vivid as its history, and whether you're peeking through a fence or touring a restored interior, you're sure to find yourself time-traveling. It's the ultimate urban treasure hunt for curious travelers, design lovers, and history buffs alike – with each address offering a little "keyhole" view into Parisian life across the centuries. Enjoy your journey through living history!

Complete List of 60+ Unique Chateaux & Houses in Paris – Sorted by Arrondissement

Place	Address	Closest Metro	Arrondissement
Château de Chantilly	Chantilly – 50 minutes from Paris by train	Gare du Nord	Suburbs
Villa Savoye	Poissy – 1 hour from Paris by train	Line J from Gare Saint-Lazare + 15-min walk	Suburbs
Château de Malmaison	Rueil-Malmaison – 30 minutes from Paris by train	Gare Saint-Lazare + short bus/Uber	Suburbs
Château de Fontainebleau	Fontainebleau – 1 hour from Paris by train	Gare de Lyon	Suburbs
Château de Vaux-le-Vicomte	Maincy – 1 hr 15 min from Paris by train	Gare de Lyon + taxi/Uber	Suburbs
Château de Rambouillet	Rambouillet – 45 min from Paris by train	Gare Montparnasse	Suburbs
Château de Maisons (a.k.a. Maisons-Laffitte)	Maisons-Laffitte – 30 minutes from Paris by train	RER A or train from Gare Saint-Lazare	Suburbs

Château de Sceaux	Sceaux – 30-40 minutes from Paris by train	RER B from central Paris	Suburbs
Château de Vincennes	Vincennes – 20 minutes from Paris by train	Metro Line 1	Suburbs
Château de Compiègne	Compiègne – 1 hr 15 min from Paris by train	Gare du Nord	Suburbs
Château de Monte-Cristo	Le Port-Marly – 1 hour from Paris by train	Gare Saint-Lazare + short walk or taxi)	Suburbs
Château de Breteuil	Choisel – 1 hour by car or 90 minutes by train + bus	Paris	Suburbs
Château de Courances	Courances – 1 hr 15 min by car; not easily accessible by public transport	--	Suburbs
Château de Dampierre-en-Yvelines	Dampierre-en-Yvelines – about 1 hour by car from Paris; limited train access + taxi	--	Suburbs

Château de Saint-Jean-de-Beauregard	Saint-Jean-de-Beauregard – 45 minutes by car; not accessible by train	--	Suburbs
Coco Chanel's Apartment	31 Rue Cambon		1st
Frédéric Chopin's Last Residence	12 Place Vendôme		1st
Colette's Palais-Royal Apartment	9 Rue de Beaujolais		1st
Nicolas Flamel's House	51 Rue de Montmorency		3rd
Hôtel Carnavalet (Musée de l'Histoire de Paris)	23 Rue de Sévigné		3rd
Musée Picasso (Hôtel Salé)	5 Rue de Thorigny		3rd
Hôtel de Soubise (Archives Nationales)	60 Rue des Francs-Bourgeois		3rd
Maison de Victor Hugo	6 Place des Vosges		4th

Hôtel de Sully	62 Rue Saint-Antoine		4th
Hôtel de Sens	1 Rue du Figuier		4th
Hôtel Lambert	2 Quai d'Anjou		4th
Hôtel de Lauzun	17 Quai d'Anjou		4th
Ernest Hemingway's First Paris Home	74 Rue du Cardinal Lemoine		5th
Paul Verlaine's Final Abode	39 Rue Descartes		5th
Gertrude Stein's Salon	27 Rue de Fleurus		6th
Oscar Wilde's Last Home (L'Hôtel)	13 Rue des Beaux-Arts		6th
Musée National Eugène Delacroix	6 Rue de Furstenberg		6th
Musée Zadkine (Sculptor's Studio)	100 bis Rue d'Assas		6th
Françoise Sagan's Apartment	34 Rue Guynemer		6th

Musée Rodin (Hôtel Biron)	77 Rue de Varenne		7th
Hôtel Matignon (Prime Minister's Residence)	57 Rue de Varenne		7th
Maison de Serge Gainsbourg	5 bis Rue de Verneuil		7th
Hôtel de Beauharnais (German Ambassador's Residence)	78 Rue de Lille		7th
Julia Child's Apartment ("Roo de Loo")	81 Rue de l'Université		7th
Musée Jacquemart-André	158 Boulevard Haussmann		8th
Musée Nissim de Camondo	63 Rue de Monceau		8th
Élysée Palace	55 Rue du Faubourg Saint-Honoré		8th
Hôtel de la Païva	25 Avenue des Champs-Élysées		8th

Musée de la Vie Romantique	16 Rue Chaptal		9th
Square d'Orléans	80 Rue Taitbout		9th
Musée Gustave Moreau	14 Rue de La Rochefoucauld		9th
Musée Édith Piaf	5 Rue Crespin-du-Gast		11th
Maison Planeix	24 bis Boulevard Masséna		13th
Villa Seurat Artists' Colony	Villa Seurat		14th
La Ruche ("The Beehive" Artists' Colony)	2 Passage Dantzig		15th
Musée Bourdelle	18 Rue Antoine Bourdelle		15th
Maison de Balzac	47 Rue Raynouard		16th
Musée Marmottan Monet	2 Rue Louis Boilly		16th

Villa La Roche (Le Corbusier Foundation)	8-10 Square du Docteur Blanche		16th
Castel Béranger	14 Rue La Fontaine		16th
Hôtel Gaillard (Cité de l'Économie)	1 Place du Général-Catroux		17th
Dalida's House	11 bis Rue d'Orchampt		18th
Le Bateau-Lavoir	13 Rue Ravignan (Place Émile-Goudeau)		18th
Musée de Montmartre & Renoir Gardens	12–14 Rue Cortot		18th
Vincent van Gogh's Montmartre Apartment	54 Rue Lepic		18th
Tristan Tzara House	15 Avenue Junot		18th

Complete List of All Locations (Quirky History, Romantic Spots and Chic Homes) – Sorted by Arrondissement

Place	Address	Closest Metro	Arrondissement
Jardin du Palais Royal	43 Rue de Valois, 75001 Paris	Palais Royal – Musée du Louvre	1st
Place Dauphine	Place Dauphine, 75001 Paris	Pont Neuf	1st
Place Vendôme	Place Vendôme, 75001 Paris	Opéra	1st
Pont Neuf	Pont Neuf, 75001 Paris	Pont Neuf	1st
Pont des Arts	Pont des Arts, 75001 Paris	Louvre – Rivoli	1st
Square du Vert-Galant	1 Square du Vert Galant, 75001 Paris	Pont Neuf	1st
Square du Vert-Galant	1 Square du Vert Galant, 75001 Paris	Pont Neuf	1st
Jardin des Tuileries -- The "Little Red Man" Ghost	Place de la Concorde, 75001 Paris	Tuileries, Concorde	1st

Point Zéro des Routes de France (Notre-Dame Parvis)	Parvis Notre-Dame, 75001 Paris	Cité	1st
Palais de Justice (includes Sainte-Chapelle)	8 Boulevard du Palais, 75001 Paris	Cité, Saint-Michel	1st
Coco Chanel's Apartment	31 Rue Cambon	Tuileries	1st
Frédéric Chopin's Last Residence	12 Place Vendôme	Opéra	1st
Colette's Palais-Royal Apartment	9 Rue de Beaujolais	Palais Royal – Musée du Louvre	1st
Galerie Vivienne	4 Rue des Petits Champs, 75002 Paris	Bourse	2nd
Rue Montorgueil	Rue Montorgueil, 75002 Paris	Sentier	2nd
12 Rue Chabanais	12 Rue Chabanais, 75002 Paris	Quatre-Septembre, Opéra	2nd

Harry's New York Bar -- Birthplace of the Bloody Mary	5 Rue Daunou, 75002 Paris	Opéra	2nd
Rue des Degrés -- The Shortest Street in Paris	Rue des Degrés, 75002 Paris	Étienne Marcel	2nd
Bibliothèque Nationale (Richelieu site) -- Marie Curie's Radioactive Notebooks	58 Rue de Richelieu, 75002 Paris	Bourse, Quatre-Septembre	2nd
Jardin Anne-Frank	14 Impasse Berthaud, 75003 Paris	Rambuteau	3rd
Square Saint-Gilles-du-Grand-Veneur	Rue de Hesse, 75003 Paris	Chemin Vert	3rd
Square du Temple – Elie Wiesel	64 Rue de Bretagne, 75003 Paris	Temple	3rd

51 Rue de Montmorency -- Nicolas Flamel's House (Alchemy Legend)	51 Rue de Montmorency, 75003 Paris	Rambuteau, Arts et Métiers	3rd
Nicolas Flamel's House	51 Rue de Montmorency	Arts et Métiers	3rd
Hôtel Carnavalet (Musée de l'Histoire de Paris)	23 Rue de Sévigné	Saint-Paul	3rd
Musée Picasso (Hôtel Salé)	5 Rue de Thorigny	Saint-Sébastien – Froissart	3rd
Hôtel de Soubise (Archives Nationales)	60 Rue des Francs-Bourgeois	Rambuteau	3rd
Au Vieux Paris d'Arcole	24 Rue Chanoinesse, 75004 Paris	Cité	4th
Hôtel de Sully Garden	62 Rue Saint-Antoine, 75004 Paris	Saint-Paul	4th
Jardin des Rosiers – Joseph-Migneret	10 Rue des Rosiers, 75004 Paris	Saint-Paul	4th

Place des Vosges	Place des Vosges, 75004 Paris	Chemin Vert	4th
Pont Marie	Pont Marie, 75004 Paris	Pont Marie	4th
Rue des Barres	Rue des Barres, 75004 Paris	Pont Marie	4th
Square Jean XXIII	4 Parvis Notre-Dame, 75004 Paris	Cité	4th
Village Saint-Paul	Rue Saint-Paul, 75004 Paris	Saint-Paul	4th
Île Saint-Louis & Place Louis Aragon	Quai de Bourbon, 75004 Paris	Pont Marie	4th
Notre-Dame Cathedral -- The Devil's Doorway (Biscornet's Wrought Iron); Relic-Filled Weathervane Survives Fire	6 Parvis Notre-Dame, 75004 Paris	Cité, Saint-Michel	4th

Rue Chanoinesse (Île de la Cité) -- Sweeney Todd of Paris (Medieval Legend)	Rue Chanoinesse, 75004 Paris	Cité	4th
Square de l'Île-de-France (Ile de la Cité)	Square de l'Île-de-France, 75004 Paris	Cité, Pont Neuf	4th
Pont Neuf -- Henry IV's Time Capsule Statue	Pont Neuf, 75004 Paris	Pont Neuf	4th
Les Innocents (Les Halles) -- The Stinking Cemetery and the Birth of the Catacombs	Place Joachim-du-Bellay, 75001 Paris	Châtelet-Les Halles	4th
Maison de Victor Hugo	6 Place des Vosges	Chemin Vert	4th
Hôtel de Sully	62 Rue Saint-Antoine	Saint-Paul	4th
Hôtel de Sens	1 Rue du Figuier	Pont Marie	4th
Hôtel Lambert	2 Quai d'Anjou	Pont Marie	4th

Hôtel de Lauzun	17 Quai d'Anjou	Pont Marie	4th
Jardin des Plantes	57 Rue Cuvier, 75005 Paris	Gare d'Austerlitz	5th
Rue Mouffetard	Rue Mouffetard, 75005 Paris	Place Monge	5th
Saint-Étienne-du-Mont	Place Sainte-Geneviève, 75005 Paris	Cardinal Lemoine	5th
Square René-Viviani	25 Quai de Montebello, 75005 Paris	Saint-Michel	5th
Arènes de Lutèce -- A Roman Arena in Paris	49 Rue Monge, 75005 Paris	Place Monge, Cardinal Lemoine	5th
René Viviani -- The Oldest Tree in Paris	Square René Viviani, 75005 Paris	Saint-Michel, Maubert-Mutualité	5th
Panthéon -- Foucault's Pendulum and Earth's Rotation	Place du Panthéon, 75005 Paris	Cardinal Lemoine, Luxembourg	5th
Rue du Chat-qui-Pêche -- Narrowest Street in Paris (and a Cat)	Rue du Chat-qui-Pêche, 75005 Paris	Saint-Michel	5th

Ernest Hemingway's First Paris Home	74 Rue du Cardinal Lemoine	Cardinal Lemoine	5th
Paul Verlaine's Final Abode	39 Rue Descartes	Place Monge	5th
Jardin du Luxembourg	Rue de Médicis – Rue de Vaugirard, 75006 Paris	Luxembourg	6th
Place de Furstenberg	Place de Furstenberg, 75006 Paris	Saint-Germain-des-Prés	6th
Le Procope (Latin Quarter) -- Napoleon's Forgotten Hat	13 Rue de l'Ancienne Comédie, 75006 Paris	Odéon	6th
Saint-Sulpice Church -- The Gnomon "Rose Line"	Place Saint-Sulpice, 75006 Paris	Saint-Sulpice	6th
Gertrude Stein's Salon	27 Rue de Fleurus	Saint-Placide	6th
Oscar Wilde's Last Home (L'Hôtel)	13 Rue des Beaux-Arts	Saint-Germain-des-Prés	6th

Musée National Eugène Delacroix	6 Rue de Furstenberg	Saint-Germain-des-Prés	6th
Musée Zadkine (Sculptor's Studio)	100 bis Rue d'Assas	Vavin	6th
Françoise Sagan's Apartment	34 Rue Guynemer	Rennes	6th
Jardin du Musée Rodin	77 Rue de Varenne, 75007 Paris	Varenne	7th
Promenade des Berges de Seine	Port de Solférino, 75007 Paris	Assemblée Nationale	7th
Rue Saint-Dominique	Rue Saint-Dominique, 75007 Paris	École Militaire	7th
Deyrolle (Rue du Bac) -- The Taxidermy Time Capsule	46 Rue du Bac, 75007 Paris	Rue du Bac	7th

Eiffel Tower -- The Man Who Sold It (Twice!); Gustave Eiffel's Secret Apartment; Saved by Science and Radio	Champ de Mars, 5 Avenue Anatole France, 75007 Paris	Bir-Hakeim, Trocadéro	7th
Luxor Obelisk (Place de la Concorde) -- The "Broken" Gift Clock	Place de la Concorde, 75008 Paris	Concorde	7th
Musée Rodin (Hôtel Biron)	77 Rue de Varenne	Varenne	7th
Hôtel Matignon (Prime Minister's Residence)	57 Rue de Varenne	Varenne	7th
Maison de Serge Gainsbourg	5 bis Rue de Verneuil	Rue du Bac	7th
Hôtel de Beauharnais (German Ambassador's Residence)	78 Rue de Lille	Solférino	7th

Julia Child's Apartment ("Roo de Loo")	81 Rue de l'Université	Pont de l'Alma	7th
Musée Jacquemart-André	158 Boulevard Haussmann, 75008 Paris	Miromesnil	8th
Parc Monceau	35 Boulevard de Courcelles, 75008 Paris	Monceau	8th
Pont Alexandre III	Pont Alexandre III, 75008 Paris	Invalides	8th
Place de la Concorde (formerly Place de la Révolution) -- Guillotine Gossip and a Blushing Head	Place de la Concorde, 75008 Paris	Concorde	8th
Flame of Liberty (Alma Bridge)	Place de l'Alma, 75008 Paris	Alma-Marceau	8th
Musée Jacquemart-André	158 Boulevard Haussmann	Miromesnil	8th
Musée Nissim de Camondo	63 Rue de Monceau	Monceau	8th

Élysée Palace	55 Rue du Faubourg Saint-Honoré	Miromesnil	8th
Hôtel de la Païva	25 Avenue des Champs-Élysées	Franklin D. Roosevelt	8th
Musée de la Vie Romantique	16 Rue Chaptal, 75009 Paris	Pigalle	9th
Musée de la Vie Romantique Garden Café	16 Rue Chaptal, 75009 Paris	Pigalle	9th
Place Saint-Georges	Place Saint-Georges, 75009 Paris	Saint-Georges	9th
Square Édouard VII	Square Édouard VII, 75009 Paris	Opéra	9th
Palais Garnier (Opéra House)	Place de l'Opéra, 75009 Paris	Opéra	9th
Musée de la Vie Romantique	16 Rue Chaptal	Pigalle	9th
Square d'Orléans	80 Rue Taitbout	Trinité – d'Estienne d'Orves	9th

Musée Gustave Moreau	14 Rue de La Rochefoucauld	Saint-Georges	9th
Canal Saint-Martin	Quai de Valmy, 75010 Paris	République	10th
145 Rue La Fayette	145 Rue La Fayette, 75010 Paris	Gare du Nord	10th
Canal Saint-Martin -- The Great Canal Cleanup and Its Sunken Treasures	Canal Saint-Martin, 75010 Paris	République	10th
Musée Édith Piaf	5 Rue Crespin-du-Gast	Ménilmontant	11th
Bois de Vincennes	Route de la Pyramide, 75012 Paris	Château de Vincennes	12th
Parc Floral de Paris	Route de la Pyramide, 75012 Paris	Château de Vincennes	12th
Promenade Plantée	1 Coulée verte René-Dumont, 75012 Paris	Bastille	12th
Rue Crémieux	Rue Crémieux, 75012 Paris	Gare de Lyon	12th

Square des Peupliers	Square des Peupliers, 75013 Paris	Tolbiac	13th
Maison Planeix	24 bis Boulevard Masséna	Porte d'Ivry	13th
Parc Montsouris	2 Rue Gazan, 75014 Paris	Cité Universitaire	14th
Paris Catacombs (Denfert-Rochereau) -- Lost Man and Haunted	1 Avenue du Colonel Henri Rol-Tanguy, 75014 Paris	Denfert-Rochereau	14th
Catacombs Concert of 1897 (Port-Mahon Gallery) -- Macabre Midnight Serenade	1 Avenue du Colonel Henri Rol-Tanguy, 75014 Paris	Denfert-Rochereau	14th
Villa Seurat Artists' Colony	Villa Seurat	Denfert-Rochereau	14th
Parc André Citroën	2 Rue Cauchy, 75015 Paris	Balard	15th
Parc Georges Brassens	2 Place Jacques Marette, 75015 Paris	Convention	15th

Petite Ceinture Trail	Entrée: 26 Rue de l'Avre, 75015 Paris	La Motte-Picquet – Grenelle	15th
Pont de Bir-Hakeim	Pont de Bir-Hakeim, 75015 Paris	Bir-Hakeim	15th
La Ruche ("The Beehive" Artists' Colony)	2 Passage Dantzig	Convention	15th
Musée Bourdelle	18 Rue Antoine Bourdelle	Montparnasse – Bienvenüe	15th
Parc de Bagatelle	Bois de Boulogne, Route de Sèvres à Neuilly, 75016 Paris	Pont de Neuilly (plus a walk or bus)	16th
Palais de Chaillot Tunnels (Trocadéro) -- The Secret 2004 Cinema	1 Place du Trocadéro, 75016 Paris	Trocadéro	16th
Maison de Balzac	47 Rue Raynouard	Passy	16th
Musée Marmottan Monet	2 Rue Louis Boilly	La Muette	16th

Villa La Roche (Le Corbusier Foundation)	8-10 Square du Docteur Blanche	Jasmin	16th
Castel Béranger	14 Rue La Fontaine	Jasmin	16th
Square des Batignolles	144bis Rue Cardinet, 75017 Paris	Brochant	17th
Hôtel Gaillard (Cité de l'Économie)	1 Place du Général-Catroux	Malesherbes	17th
Hôtel Particulier Montmartre	23 Avenue Junot, 75018 Paris	Lamarck–Caulaincourt	18th
La Maison Rose	2 Rue de l'Abreuvoir, 75018 Paris	Lamarck–Caulaincourt	18th
Montmartre Vineyards	14–18 Rue des Saules, 75018 Paris	Lamarck–Caulaincourt	18th
Place des Abbesses	Place des Abbesses, 75018 Paris	Abbesses	18th
Rue Lepic	Rue Lepic, 75018 Paris	Abbesses	18th
Square Louise Michel	6 Place Saint-Pierre, 75018 Paris	Abbesses	18th

Square Marcel Bleustein-Blanchet	Rue de la Bonne, 75018 Paris	Abbesses	18th
Place Marcel-Aymé (Montmartre)	Place Marcel-Aymé, 75018 Paris	Abbesses, Lamarck-Caulaincourt	18th
Place Dalida (Montmartre) -- The Shiny-Bosomed Bust	Place Dalida, 75018 Paris	Lamarck-Caulaincourt	18th
Clos Montmartre (Montmartre)	Rue des Saules, 75018 Paris	Rue des Saules, 75018 Paris	18th
Moulin de la Galette (Montmartre)	83 Rue Lepic, 75018 Paris	Abbesses, Lamarck-Caulaincourt	18th
Moulin Rouge (Pigalle) -- Le Pétomane: The Fartiste of Montmartre	82 Boulevard de Clichy, 75018 Paris	Blanche, Pigalle	18th

Théâtre du Grand-Guignol (Pigalle) (Note: Theatre no longer exists, but was in this area)	20 bis Rue Chaptal, 75009 Paris	Pigalle, Saint-Georges	18th
Dalida's House	11 bis Rue d'Orchampt	Lamarck – Caulaincourt	18th
Le Bateau-Lavoir	13 Rue Ravignan (Place Émile-Goudeau)	Abbesses	18th
Musée de Montmartre & Renoir Gardens	12–14 Rue Cortot	Lamarck – Caulaincourt	18th
Vincent van Gogh's Montmartre Apartment	54 Rue Lepic	Blanche	18th
Tristan Tzara House	15 Avenue Junot	Lamarck – Caulaincourt	18th
Parc de la Villette	211 Avenue Jean Jaurès, 75019 Paris	Porte de Pantin	19th
Parc des Buttes-Chaumont	1 Rue Botzaris, 75019 Paris	Buttes-Chaumont	19th

Parc de Belleville	47 Rue des Couronnes, 75020 Paris	Couronnes	20th
Père Lachaise Cemetery -- The Fertility Grave of Victor Noir	16 Rue du Repos, 75020 Paris	Père Lachaise, Philippe Auguste	20th
Mur des Fédérés (Père Lachaise) -- The Communards' Last Stand	16 Rue du Repos, 75020 Paris	Père Lachaise, Philippe Auguste	20th